Aminta

A Pastoral Play

Aminta

A Pastoral Play

by

Torquato Tasso

Edited and Translated by
Charles Jernigan and
Irene Marchegiani Jones

Italica Press
New York
2000

Italica Press Dual-language Poetry Series

ITALICA PRESS, INC.
595 Main Street
New York, New York 10044

Library of Congress Cataloging-in-Publication Data
Tasso, Torquato, 1544–1595.
[Aminta. English & Italian]
Aminta: a pastoral play / by Torquato Tasso; edited and translated by Charles Jernigan and Irene Marchegiani Jones.
p. cm. — (Italica press dual-language poetry series)
Includes bibliographical references.
ISBN 978-0-934977-65-4 (trade pbk: alk. paper)
I. Jernigan, Charles, 1942– II. Jones, Irene Marchegiani. III. Title. IV. Series.

PQ4642.E22 J47 2000
852'.4—dc21

00-063221

ISBN: 978-0-934977-65-4

Printed in the U.S.A and E.U.
5 4 3 2

Cover art and illustrations in text from Aldine Press edition of Aminta (Venice, 1589). By permission of the Biblioteca Panizzi, Comune di Reggio Emilia.

About the Editors and Translators

Charles Jernigan is Chair of the Department of Comparative Literature and Classics at California State University, Long Beach. He has served several times as Director of the California State University study abroad Program in Florence, Italy. His publications include articles on medieval and Renaissance Italian literature and on Italian opera. He is currently translating Emilia Branca's biography of her husband, the librettist Felice Romani.

Irene Marchegiani Jones is Professor of Italian at California State University, Long Beach. She has written articles on Giacomo Leopardi and modern and contemporary Italian literature, with particular interest in women writers. In collaboration with Carol Lettieri she has translated *Star of Free Will* by Maria Luisa Spaziani and *Angels of Youth* by Luigi Fontanella. She has also published some of her poetry in Italian journals. She is co-editor (with Tom Haeussler) of *The Poetics of Place: Florence Imagined.* Her scholarly interests are also related to the teaching of the Italian language and she is co-author of the Italian reader *Incontri Attuali* and the texbook *Crescendo!*

To
Nicole and Geoff Jernigan
Arianna and Olivia Jones

Contents

Introduction

Torquato Tasso's *Aminta* is a masterpiece and perhaps the most famous pastoral play ever written. It was created in the sixteenth century during a period when the Greek and Latin classics exercised enormous fascination in Italy. In the late Renaissance, under the influence of idyllic and Arcadian literary forms, pastoral fables, simple in structure and evoking graceful myths in the form of dialogic eclogues, became popular. Pastoral literature tended to idealize the unsophisticated, innocent, and serene lives of shepherds in contrast to complex and frequently corrupt city life. The archetypal paradigm of this life was the Golden Age, a mythical, utopian time when human beings were content with their simple, peaceful lives, and when the uncultivated earth offered them everything they needed. The myth of the Golden Age, already present in the Greek poet Hesiod, is later treated by, among others, the great Roman poet Virgil.

I. The Pastoral Form and Its Origins

A fundamental characteristic of the pastoral drama is its natural setting, often a forest where the characters are "rustic" types, usually shepherds and nymphs who live simply, but who express very urban sentiments in sophisticated language. Pastoral or bucolic (from the Greek βουκολοζ, shepherd) poetry was originally mostly in the form of idylls (poems describing the charming life in the countryside) or eclogues (a soliloquy or dialogue spoken by shepherds). During the Renaissance, however, eclogue designated all poetic works with a pastoral setting, such as Edmund Spenser's *The Shepherd's Calendar* (1579).

Both the idyll and the eclogue had their origin in Greek bucolic poetry—bucolic in the sense of a sentimental view of nature, as in the idyllic and romantic descriptions of a countryside for which the poet longs as an escape from city life. These elements, present in Euripides and Plato, are a central component of Theocritus' *Idylls* and are a consequence of the noisy, dirty, complex life in big urban centers in the third century B.C.E. As in other eras boasting a refined culture, Hellenistic Greece represented the countryside as the sweet counterpoise to hectic city life; people who were tired of working and overwhelmed by urban culture and lifestyle, looked for peace and relief in the country, which was pictured in the poetry as being primitive and natural, but also conventional and stylized.

Although pastoral components can be found in the poetry of early Greek lyric poets like Stesichorus and Ibycus, the invention of true pastoral poetry is usually attributed to Theocritus (fl. 270 B.C.E.), whose *Idylls* provide models for the pastoral. Virgil derived the splendid poetry of his *Eclogues* from Theocritus. In the *Eclogues* the countryside and shepherds are not presented in a realistic manner, the scenery is pure fantasy, and the entire landscape and environment are a creation of the poet's mind and imagination.

In the early Renaissance, Giovanni Boccaccio's *Ameto,* a sort of novel interspersed with poems, can be considered a pastoral work, but it is really Iacopo Sannazaro's *Arcadia* that for centuries has been considered as the embodiment and culmination of the bucolic tradition. Arcadia was the region of ancient Greece which served as a setting for many pastorals, and Sannazaro took the name of his pastoral "novel," published in 1504, from that association. Here the author gives the traditionally unrelated eclogues or pastoral poems a unifying story line.

It was from this Arcadian ideal, this bucolic tradition that a new genre, pastoral drama, would arise and flourish during the Renaissance: it is a form that was part and parcel of the classicizing atmosphere of the times and it takes the form of eclogues in dialogic form. The genre had found expression as early as Angelo Poliziano's *Orfeo* (1471), perhaps the first of the Renaissance pastoral plays presented on stage to accompany courtly celebrations. The dialogic pastoral poem with its relatively free structure developed into a stricter five-act format, the meter of which was usually hendecasyllabic (eleven syllable) blank verse punctuated by more lyrical, often rhymed, choral songs. Various attempts were made to codify this structure, notably by Giraldi Cinzio with his *Egle* and *Favola Pastorale*, by Luigi Tansillo with *Pellegrini*, and by Agostino Beccari with *Il Sacrificio*; but it is only with Torquato Tasso's *Aminta* (1573) and later Battista Guarini's *Il Pastor Fido* (1590) that the pastoral drama acquired a place in the poetic canon, a place between the dialogic eclogue and the developing melodrama.

II. Plot and Characters

The plot of *Aminta* is deceptively simple. A young shepherd, Aminta, loves a nymph named Silvia; she, a devout follower of Diana, goddess of chastity and the hunt, rejects his suit. Aminta is distraught, and he is counseled by two older characters, his fellow shepherd Tirsi and an ex-follower of Diana, Dafne. When Silvia announces that she is going to bathe in Diana's spring to wash away the "sweat and dust" (1.1.237) from yesterday's hunt to prepare for a new one, Dafne and Tirsi tell Aminta to go there and confront her when she is "alone and nude" (3.2.35). They expect that nature will take its course, and Dafne even suggests that if Silvia does not yield willingly, Aminta can take her by force.

Meanwhile, a lustful satyr also has designs on Silvia, and since she is even less likely to yield to him, he plots rape. When Aminta and Tirsi arrive at Diana's spring, they see the nude Silvia bound to a tree with her own hair, and the satyr about to rape her. Aminta, "just like a lion" (3.1.70), chases the satyr away with Tirsi's help and frees Silvia. Rather than being grateful, she speaks harshly to him and dashes off into the wood. Dafne prevents the grieving Aminta from committing suicide and is busy telling him to "live on / in your deep wretchedness" (3.2.21–22) when Nerina, another nymph, appears with disconcerting news. Silvia has come to her home to dress and together they have gone to rendezvous for the planned hunt; right away a wolf appeared and Silvia shot at him, wounding him. The wolf rushed off into the woods and Silvia dashed off after him, with Nerina following. Tracing Silvia's footprints to a spot deep in the forest, Nerina sees Silvia's arrow and a veil she was using to tie her hair, and soon she sees a pack of wolves busy eating the last flesh from a pile of bones.

Aminta, like Nerina, immediately assumes that Silvia has been eaten by wolves. When Nerina refuses to give him Silvia's veil, which he wants to use to hang himself, he rushes off to commit suicide by throwing himself from a rocky cliff. In Act 4 we learn that Silvia is alive and well. The wolves had been devouring the "body of a beast" (4.1.18); Silvia lost her veil while she was fleeing the wounded wolf, which once again she failed to kill. When she has told Dafne her story, Dafne tells her that Aminta, believing her dead, has gone off to kill himself; for the first time Silvia feels some emotion towards him and wants to run after him and save him. Now Ergasto, another denizen of the countryside, arrives with the tale that Aminta has thrown himself from a cliff onto the rocks below, killing himself. Ergasto, in trying to stop him, has grabbed at him, but has only the "soft and silken band / that circled him" (4.2.105) to show for his attempt. Silvia, now truly distraught, feels compassion and guilt, and sets off to find and bury Aminta's body, and then, presumably, to end her own life by hanging herself with Aminta's "band."

The last act resolves the plot happily. The wise shepherd Elpino tells us that Aminta has not died; his fall was broken by some bushes, and though bruised and at first unconscious, he is not badly hurt. Silvia is with him, "curing" him with kisses, and Elpino is on his way to find her father Montano to bless their union.

Simply put, boy loves girl who disdains him. He threatens suicide, and when he thinks she has been killed by animals, he tries to kill himself. She is moved to compassion, and eventually love, by his act, and when it is discovered that the report of his death is premature, as the report of hers has been, they are happily united in blissful, erotic love.

The characters in *Aminta* are the traditional "rustic" types inherited from the ancient Greek and Roman pastoral tradition as well as from Renaissance models. Just as the setting for the pastoral is nature—the fields and the forests—rather than the city, so the characters who populate the natural setting are its personages, particularly shepherds and nymphs. In ancient mythology, nymphs were rather like minor goddesses inhabiting forests, meadows, mountains, and rivers, but in the Renaissance they have become devotees of pagan goddesses. Silvia is dedicated to Diana, goddess of chastity and the hunt. The shepherds too have special relationships to the more rustic or "country" gods, witness Aminta's prayer to Pomona, Pan, Pallas, and Priapus (a curious country quadrivium of field and fecundity) before he leaps to his supposed death. Otherwise, the chief characteristics of these folk are their absorption by love, their simplicity, and their ability to express themselves in often ornate and courtly language infused with rhetorical devices. This was, of course, court drama, and these "simple rustics" are really courtiers in the attire of country characters, an idea that reached its apogee at the end of the eighteenth century when Marie Antoinette had a country village constructed for herself on the back-lot of Versailles so that she could play dress up and pretend to be a milkmaid.

III. The d'Estes

The d'Este family had governed Ferrara since the fourteenth century and their court had become one of the jewels of Renaissance Europe. Alberto d'Este (1347–1393) began the transformation of the city. In 1393 he established the university, and his son Niccolò d'Este (1383–1441), a great patron of the arts, particularly music, built the castle that still dominates Ferrara. Leonello (1407–1450), who succeeded Niccolò, was well educated in the classics, philosophy, and history, while Borso d'Este (1413–1471) was more interested in law and medicine and provided great support for the university. The daughter of Ercole d'Este (1431–1505), Isabella, became one of the leading figures of the Italian Renaissance and an outstanding patron of the arts following her marriage to the Marquis of Mantua. Isabella, born in 1474, inherited her father's passion for the arts as well as for building, theater, and travel. An extremely accomplished woman, once in Mantua she became her father's competitor in collecting art.

It was mostly under Isabella's father Ercole and his son Alfonso I d'Este (1476–1534), who married Lucrezia Borgia, that Ferrara became one of the strongest political powers and cultural centers as the d'Estes patronized artists from all over Italy and Europe. Writers and poets like Pietro Bembo and Ludovico Ariosto lived at their court. Ariosto, author of the chivalric epic *Orlando Furioso,* first worked for Cardinal Ippolito d'Este, who built the spectacular gardens of the Villa d'Este at Tivoli, near Rome, and later for Duke Alfonso. Alfonso, like his successor Ercole II (1508–1559), particularly supported music, spending great sums on Italian and foreign musicians and composers. Alfonso's wife Lucrezia Borgia also became one of the most influential patrons of the arts, often contending with her sister-in-law Isabella in supporting artists.

Among the many great writers who were attracted by the d'Estes was Torquato Tasso, who began working in the household of Cardinal Luigi d'Este in 1565 and eventually joined the court under Alfonso II in 1572.

IV. The Play and the d'Este Court

A part of the pastoral tradition is that "common folk," to use Cupid's words, are really aristocrats in disguise, and much of the pleasure of those early aristocratic audiences must have been in seeing people they knew depicted and sometimes satirized under the guise of shepherds and nymphs. Tasso puts several of the fixtures of the d'Este court in the play, and most important of those court figures is Tasso himself, under the guise of the poet–shepherd Tirsi. As has often been pointed out, Tirsi is twenty-nine, exactly the age of Tasso when *Aminta* was written and produced in 1573; Dafne even warns Tirsi not to "put...down in rhyme" (2.2.96) what she has told him about "how woman is designed" (2.2.90), so obviously Tirsi–Tasso is a poet too. Tirsi has inherited his "shepherd's pipes" from "that great man who sang of arms and loves" (1.1.192), that is, Tasso is in line to become heir of Ariosto, who earlier in the century had brought fame and glory to the d'Este court with the *Orlando Furioso* and other works. Tirsi even tells us that he has been asked to return "to these retreats" and lay aside for awhile the "trumpet tones" he used to sing "of wars and men" (1.2.299–306), a clear reference to Tasso's great epic poem, the *Gerusalemme liberata,* which he had begun as early as 1565. Through Tirsi, he tells us here that he has been requested to write a pastoral play. We may also assume that Tasso is speaking through Tirsi when he tells Dafne that although he has given up love, he has not given up "Venus' joys" since he prefers to have "love's sweet without the bitterness" (2.2.129–30). Tasso never married.

Much contemporary criticism on the *Aminta* concerns the relation of the play to the d'Este court, both to its personages and to its setting. The wise Elpino is usually seen as the poet Giovanni Battista Pigna, secretary to Duke Alfonso II d'Este, while the Licori, referred to in 1.1.184 and in Act 5 (5.1.65), is Lucrezia Bendidio, lady-in-waiting to Eleonora d'Este and object of youthful love poetry by Tasso. Most of the modern criticism in this vein, however, has centered on Tirsi's "Mopso Speech" (1.2.228–315) —what a certain Mopso has told him about the evils of the court, which Tirsi refutes. Mopso (who does not appear in the play) is generally held to be Sperone Speroni, Aristotelian philosopher and critic, who tried to dissuade Tasso from returning to court. Alfonso II himself is in the speech as "a guard of things so fine and rare" (1.2.281); there may also be references to the d'Este princesses Eleonora and Lucrezia and to their ladies-in-waiting, and there are certainly references to Tasso's fellow court poets, particularly Giovan Battista Pigna and Battista Guarini, who is called Batto in the *Aminta,* author of the other great pastoral play of Renaissance Italy, the *Pastor Fido.*

The "grotto of Aurora" mentioned in 1.1.187 and described in Tirsi's "Mopso Speech" (1.2.290) probably refers to a famous room in the ducal palace in Ferrara, which still exists and which contains a fresco by Dosso Dossi depicting Aurora. Some critics feel that the setting of *Aminta* is actually the island of Belvedere in the Po River, where the first performance may have taken place. Thus several of the characters and some of the settings within the play and for the play were probably real. While a modern audience does not really need to know all this, it adds an additional dimension to the play, which the original audience would have found amusing and which links the rustics in the play to the sophisticates in the audience in a manner that adds to an ironic tone which permeates much of the play.

Additionally, certain passages were added by Tasso after 1573; some were originally used for other purposes, including the choruses that conclude Acts 3 and 4. The "Mopso Speech," which most clearly concerns the d'Este court, was also apparently a later addition. These extrinsic pieces, which include the *intermedii* (interludes), suggest an additional level of court-play relations and make the court audience active participants in the pastoral goings-on. Tirsi's "Mopso Speech" (1.2.228–315) in particular pulls the court into the play.

Mopso, as said before, was probably Sperone Speroni, whom the young Tasso had studied with in Padua; he is supposed to have warned Tasso against joining the court at Ferrara, just as Mopso has nothing good to say about "the city [that] sits upon the river's bank" (1.2.233) and particularly "the shop of nothing-is" (1.2.245), which would seem to be the court or the ducal palace itself. The duke's "shop," it seems, is a place where nothing is what it seems to be and everyone is out to get you—probably not a bad description of a Renaissance court, and one that the paranoid Tasso would certainly have reason to believe true before the 1570s ended. Tirsi, however, turns Sperone/Mopso's warning into a generous compliment for his patron Alfonso II and tells us that while there he was able to "...become a greater man / infused with newfound strength...and sang of wars and men,...with...trumpet tones" (1.2.297–306), a clear reference to the *Gerusalemme.* Mopso, however, fixed Tirsi "with his evil stare," which made him "hoarse and silent for a long, long time" (1.2.307–8). This is perhaps an allusion to Tasso's confinement in Sant'Anna Hospital after 1579 or to his earlier "house arrest," if the speech was added to the play in the 1580s.

Thus court figures and events loom large among the pastoral characters and circumstances of the *Aminta.* Just as Virgil had praised his patron under the name of Pollio in one of his pastoral works, the *Fourth Eclogue,* and predicted that Pollio's newborn son would eventually usher in a Golden Age, so Tasso makes the court scene a part of his pastoral drama. One does not have to know much about these historical connections to read or enjoy *Aminta,* but it certainly contributes to the curious tone of the play, both distancing the play's events and linking them to the real world.

V. Reception and Influence

Most modern critics feel that *Aminta* was written in Spring 1573 and first performed on July 31 by the Gelosi company on the island of Belvedere del Po, near Ferrara; the d'Este summer palace was situated there. No account of that first performance survives, but the following year the play was performed in Pesaro at the behest of Lucrezia d'Este, who had married Francesco Maria della Rovere, prince of nearby Urbino, in 1570. An account of that performance survives, and it apparently "brought great pleasure to the spectators." *Aminta,* in fact, made Tasso's reputation, and it was performed successfully several times in the next years, in locales that would not necessarily have been privy to the inside references. It was not published until 1581 by Aldo Manuzio's press in Venice when Tasso was already confined in Sant'Anna Hospital. At virtually the same time it was published in Cremona, and numerous other editions followed, including the Aldine (after Aldo Manuzio) editions of 1583, 1589, and 1590. The latter edition is the basis for B. T. Sozzi's critical edition published in 1957.

Aminta

In 1584 *Aminta* was printed in Paris, first in Italian and later that same year in a French translation. In 1591 it was printed in London and translated/adapted into English by Abraham Fraunce. There were three English translations in the seventeenth century, including the excellent one by Henry Reynolds (1628). Leigh Hunt translated it in 1820, and four translations into English came out in the twentieth century, including an Internet version by Malcolm Hayward (1997). Hunt's version was reprinted in 1964 in *The Genius of the Italian Theater,* edited by Eric Bentley, and Reynold's version was reprinted in 1991 in *Tasso's* Aminta *and Other Poems,* edited by Glyn Pursglove, and in 1993 in *Three Renaissance Pastorals: Tasso—Guarini—Daniel,* edited by Elizabeth Story Donno. Besides French and English, it has been translated into Latin, Spanish, Dutch, Danish, Polish, Hungarian, Slavic–Illinic, and Greek.

Aminta's influence has been phenomenal, spawning in Italy alone over 200 plays by 1700. Spenser seems to have been inspired by it, and the Italian pastoral is the source of numerous plays in France, Spain and England, and, indirectly at least, it is a source of William Shakespeare's pastoral comedies such as *As You Like It, Twelfth Night,* and *A Midsummer Night's Dream,* and it is a source of John Milton's *Comus.* In Spain its influence can be traced in Tirso di Molina's *Trickster of Seville,* the first Don Juan play, and even in Miguel de Cervantes, who wrote a pastoral drama himself (the *Galeoto*) and included pastoral episodes in *Don Quixote.* In France, Antoine de Montchrestien's *Bergerie* shows close adherence to Tasso, and the pastoral remained a popular form there well into the eighteenth century.

As a stage play, *Aminta* never really ceased to be performed after its initial success in Ferrara (1573), Pesaro (1574), Mantua (1586), and Florence (1590), although its fortune has varied throughout the centuries. Performances have often been outdoors in natural settings that emphasized an interpretation of the play as symbolic of pristine life and the simple, spontaneous origin of love. For example, *Aminta* was performed in the Roman theater in Fiesole in 1914 and in the Boboli Gardens in Florence in 1939, in the courtyard of the Ducal Palace in Urbino in 1952, and in a palace courtyard in Ferrara in 1954. After various performances in the 1950s,

Aminta lay dormant until 1994, when it was directed by the eminent Luca Ronconi. A post-modern version is currently (2000) touring in Italy and elsewhere.

Modern criticism, while not voluminous, has taken several approaches. In the late nineteenth century there was a concerted effort to establish sources for the play in Italian and ancient literature, the so-called "pastoral debates." On one side critics argued that Tasso created a new genre, while others argued that he was simply tapping into a long-viable tradition. Some contemporary critics, such as Jane Tylus Klein, have continued to examine sources. Others have continued to mine the influence of *Aminta* in other traditions, including English literature (Brand, Entzminger, Shore). Several studies have looked at the relationship between the play and the court (e.g., Jepson, Stampino), while Richard Cody places Tasso's work in the context of Renaissance Neoplatonism, and G. A. Niccoli has comparatively studied some of the archetypal features (Cupid, the satyr, the Golden Age) in Tasso, Guarini, and Montchrestien.

VI. Literary Analysis

Looking at this wonderful old work at the beginning of a new century, one is struck by the continuing problem in interpreting its subject matter. The central subject is, of course, love. Cupid introduces the play and states that this is the subject, and love is virtually the only subject of conversation among the shepherds and nymphs, and it is the generator of all the action. Yet in a love story, two things are very odd: the lovers are never shown together, and the message regarding love is ambivalent at best.

The problem in deciphering exactly what Tasso is saying about love probably comes from the essential ambivalence of the play and perhaps of the pastoral form itself. Dafne's early attempt to get Silvia to yield to love by arguing that animals, birds, snakes, and even plants respond to love draws this response: "Well, when I hear the sighs / escape the plants that woo, / then I'll be glad to be a lover too" (1.1.167–69). Tirsi's high-flown, overly dramatic rhetoric at the end of a passage praising his patron (2.2.179–204) leads Dafne to reply, "Oh, ho! You're flying high! Come on, descend..." (2.2.205). On another occasion Dafne tells Silvia about a time when the lovesick Tirsi wandered through the woods like a madman "so that the gracious nymphs and shepherds there / were moved to pity and to laugh at once" (1.1.223–24), and this seems to be our cue as audience as to how to respond to the play, which is self-ironizing. Surely the sophisticated court audiences of the late sixteenth century would have found some of the excesses of Aminta and Silvia as risible as we do.

How seriously are we to take the play? Is it comedy or tragedy? Well, neither and both. The tone is both sophisticated and simple, at times full of complex poetic rhetoric, and at times rustic or almost colloquial. Unlettered shepherds speak like courtiers and are, in fact, poets. The genre and the tone are difficult to pin down because they keep shifting and on some occasions are tragic and comic, high and low at the same time.

The tone and genre are matched by ambivalence in regard to the characters and plot. What else would you get when you array the formal classical concept of Cupid in "shepherd's humble garb" (Prologue, l. 2)? Thus is Cupid off not to escape Venus' power, "but...a mother's badgering" (Prologue, l. 30), and in disguise. Even the lustful satyr who plots to rape Silvia garners some sympathy when he argues that his only fault is being poor and that his gifts are scorned. What is this? Can't we even trust a lustful satyr to be villainous?

This is a play of disguises where nothing is what it seems to be: Cupid is disguised; Aminta collects a kiss from Silvia with a ruse; Dafne and Tirsi concoct a plan to surprise the unsuspecting Silvia; everyone believes Silvia to be dead; everyone believes Aminta to be dead. The confusion of disguise, ruse, and misunderstanding extends to the secondary themes of the play. The wonderful and justly famous chorus on the Golden Age, which ends Act 1 and which celebrates that "first fair age" (1.2.319) when there was no strife and natural law ruled and free love reigned is immediately countered by the satyr at the start of Act 2, when he argues that "this is rightly called the golden age, / since gold alone can conquer and can reign" (2.1.57–58). Is Tasso attacking the new Golden Age in Ferrara where everything is up for sale? What is the Golden Age? From the satyr's point of view, natural law licenses him to have sex with Silvia.

Even the passages that offer praise to Tasso's patron are open to question. The famous "Mopso Speech" gives 42 lines to Mopso's negative version of court life and almost exactly the same number of lines to Tirsi's rebuttal. Tirsi's extravagant praise of his patron and his gracious thanks for the leisure to do his work is mocked by Dafne, as pointed out before. Just what Tasso's view was has been the subject of numerous monographs, and the future course of his life shows a real love–hate relationship with the d'Este court. Ambivalence is the key.

No wonder that Proteus is the speaker of the first interlude that accompanied the dances between Acts 1 and 2 since he personifies changeableness. The *Aminta* is like the protean sea, always in flux and never fixed in regard to genre, tone, topical commentary, and theme. The main theme of the work is, of course, love—in all its changeableness. In a sense the characters, undefined except for their attitudes towards love, represent its various aspects. Silvia is until the end a devotee of Diana, disdains love, and represents chastity. Her opposite is the satyr, who represents unbridled lust. They are like the bookends of Aphrodite and Artemis in Euripides' *Hippolytus,* and between lie the attitudes of the others: Dafne is an older Silvia, experienced, and more than a little cynical. She counsels that women mean the opposite of what they say in matters of love and that if they persist in being unyielding, they should be taken by force. Tirsi, likewise, is in regard to this theme an older Aminta, and he seems to want sex without love:

> The man who gives up love does not give up
> all Venus' joys; he gathers up and tastes
> love's sweet without the bitterness. (2.2.128–30)

He has been burned before: "I've wept enough already, sighed enough; / let others have their share"(2.2.145–46); and yet he seems to want Dafne herself, though she toys with him. He falls in with her plan to have Aminta surprise Silvia while she is bathing, much to his later regret. Elpino is the personification of wise resignation, waiting for Licori to love him. As for Aminta, he is the very soul of the moaning, adolescent lover, unsatisfied until the end. But he is also Tasso's faithful shepherd, and his feeling is deeper than lust. He will not take advantage of Silvia; he is in love. In a sense all of these characters reflect different attitudes towards love, or perhaps the attitudes of a single person at different times and in differing circumstances, and except for Silvia they are unchanging.

The choruses that conclude each act are also about love, and they reflect different attitudes. The first one, the Golden Age chorus, argues for a sort of free love, untouched by honor when "nature's law of gold / and joy, *'do what pleases you,'* was told" (1.2.343–44): *"S'ei piace, ei lice"* in Tasso's Italian. It argues against the puritanizing effects of honor and asks that the "Lord of Love and Natural Right" (1.2.373) shake up the great and highborn and "...let us live and go / the happy way that lived the men of old" (1.2.279–80). The second act chorus is a paean to rustic love and mocks those who hope to find love's intent in "Socratic argument": "O worthy master, Love, / lord of yourself alone, / for you alone can teach us of your own" (2.3.124–26). The third act chorus approaches the Renaissance Neoplatonic idea that human love is a step on the ladder to the divine: "finding love, we also often find / immortal glory close behind" (3.2.151–52). And the fourth act chorus continues that idea with wonderful lines: "as if you, by supernal worth, inspire / mere man to soar in an immortal gyre" (4.2.204–5). Love can move us to reach immortality, which is an idea fairly similar to the great dissertation on love at the conclusion of the *Book of the Courtier.* And yet the final chorus playfully argues that they don't want to go through what Aminta has endured to find happiness: "I'd rather win my nymph / with brief entreaties and with service brief" (5.1.150–51).

So where is Tasso in the love debate? Does he side with free love and sex unfettered by codes of conduct (a position that makes a number of contemporary critics nervous)? Or does he believe that love has the power to so ennoble us that we can reach immortality through human love? (A more congenial point of view for modern Puritans.) Or does he just want a little good country lovin' with its "games of gentle scorn / and sweet refusals, and / affrays and quarrels, which cease / and yield to hearts rejoined in truce and peace" (5.1.155–58)?

Perhaps he never answers the question definitively because love is simply too changeable a topic—too protean —to pin down. He does, however, add something to the debate, which changes the whole tone, which anchors the light comedy and gentle jesting and adds a measure of tragic irony to the comic irony: the omnipresence of death.

Death or the threat of death grounds the bantering and the complaining over unrequited love and makes the play more than an inside courtly joke. The theme is sounded in the first lines of Act 1 when Dafne poses the central *carpe diem* question to Silvia (1.1.1–3): "You would, then, really, Silvia, / waste all the passing youthful years / far from the pleasures Venus offers us?" The chorus on the Golden Age, which ends the act, also asks that question and ties its answer to another prime theme of Renaissance literature from Petrarch to Cervantes and Shakespeare—the longing for a time when men and women lived naturally in an atmosphere of mutual satisfaction and love. In that Edenic environment clothes were superfluous, simple sincerity rather than fashion dictated words and actions, and honor (meaning chastity, duty, and social propriety) was unknown. Honor, in fact, has ruined everything. But a return to that Golden Age when:

> the virgin maid, undressed,
> disclosed her dewy rose,
> which now we veil and close,
> and showed the unpicked apples of her breast;
> and oft in lake and stream
> her lover frolicking with her was seen. (1.2.352–57)

would not solve the problem of mutability, which echoes in the tragic cry at the end of the chorus:

> Let's love, for Day will die, yet is reborn;
> for us, though, all its light
> sinks down, and sleep leads to eternal night.
> (1.2.384–86)

The *carpe diem* cry "Let's love" was heard among the ancient Romans (and among the Greeks before that), but it finds particular poignancy and frequency in the Renaissance, and inspired some of its greatest poetry.

Likewise the beautiful lines of the "older" (she must be over 30) and experienced Dafne in Act 2, scene 2, ll. 72–73, when she is talking to Tirsi, "Il mondo invecchia, / ed invecchiando intristisce" ("This world of ours grows old, / and growing old, grows sad) bear great world weariness. The Golden Age is gone forever. Nothing lasts except change, and maturing means the knowledge of death.

Behind all the lamenting in *Aminta* there is the tragic knowledge of death, the brevity of life, and the fact that human beings have only one consolation in the face of the inevitable: not religion, as the Middle Ages would have posited, but love—human, sensual love. Those choruses that end Acts 3 and 4 reaffirm this idea. "We don't need death at all" (3.2.144) argues the chorus at the end of Act 3; love is much better, it is:

> grace obtained by loving well.
> And finding love we also often find
> immortal glory close behind. (3.2.150–52)

The chorus at the end of Act 4 takes it one step farther, saying that love is the opposite of death and binds its wounds: "What death destroys, you, Love, make anew." It has the power to remove all hate and anger:

> as if you, by supernal worth, inspire
> mere man to soar in an immortal gyre. (4.2.204–5)

Understood in this way, the naive complications of the plot, which first require Aminta to believe that Silvia is dead, and then require Silvia to believe the same of Aminta, become clear. The knowledge of death matures us and causes us to take fate into our own hands, and act. The knowledge of Juliet's supposed death, like Silvia's, causes Romeo to cry out, "Then I defy you, stars," and to act; and Juliet acts in an equally decisive way on learning that Romeo has died, and pastoral becomes tragedy. So the news of Aminta's "death" causes Silvia to realize the frivolity of her former pursuits, while Silvia's "death" causes Aminta to set out to do what he has been threatening all along. Indeed, the reason he tries to kill himself is not Silvia's rejection—that had only caused masochistic groaning and threats of suicide—but to "follow" her, as he tells Ergasto before he throws himself from the precipice to be with her after death. It is the same attempt to achieve the "immortal gyre" through love that Juliet makes, and that Romeo has already made. Death, or the threat thereof, makes us realize that the only thing in the whole world that really matters is love. It is our bulwark against death and change, our knowledge that nothing lasts.

It is not important that Silvia and Aminta never appear together on stage. The story is not about them; it is about love, the transforming power of love, the protean transforming power of love, which can make unlettered rustics talk like court ladies and gentlemen, which can turn misery to joy, and which can perhaps link mere mortals to immortal spheres. In a world where ambivalence reigns, where nothing is fixed, and mutability is the rule, love offers us an anchor. The final glimpse we have of Aminta and Silvia, thanks to Elpino, is the Golden Age reborn, free of honor-induced shame:

> shame restrains a love that's weak,
> but it's a weak restraint for potent love. (5.1.108–9)

Aminta and his love are lying together kissing when last we see them, firmly grounded in each other and in love:

> and so conjoined [they] lay and loved as one....
> Who serves great Love will know it for himself.
> But one who doesn't know, much less can tell.
> (5.1.126–28)

Love's mystery is only known by its adherents. Those who haven't experienced it will not understand. The cynic in us can smile along with the final chorus, but the picture we come away with is of Aminta's sighs, finally "gathered up / by [Silvia's] sweet lips" (5.1.119–20), and like that chorus, we might, a little jealously, long for the "contentment" of "…hearts rejoined in truce and peace" (5.1.153–58), free, at least for an eternal moment, from the ravages of change and death.

VII. About the Translation

Although there are no major textual problems in translating *Aminta,* there is always a choice that must be made in rendering poetry into another language, and *Aminta* is in poetic form. Most of the play is in endecasyllabic blank verse, with variations of seven or eight syllable lines, and the choruses that end the acts are rhymed. We decided to "transmit" the play into English iambic pentameter blank verse (with shorter trimeter and tetrameter lines when Tasso varies the length of his own lines), and when the original rhymes, to offer a rhymed English version that follows the original rhyme scheme.

Critical interpretations of *Aminta* have been numerous and various over the years, but a given fact has always been that the poetic language is central to the work. We strove to reproduce the musicality and elegance of the original wherever possible, balancing our translation between the respect due to the archaic sixteenth-century original and a commitment towards contemporary readers. While keeping the meaning, tone, and content, we have tried to confer the musical and harmonious sound inherent in the original (and occasionally the colloquial tone as well), although we humbly admit that we are not Tasso and that the very greatness of his poetry presents real challenges to anyone who sets out to translate it. The old song says, "I've been true to you, darling, in my fashion," and we hope that our fidelity to Tasso has been sufficient.

Introduction

There is no autograph manuscript of *Aminta,* and Tasso himself seems to have made changes in it between the time of the first performance and the first (unauthorized) printed edition eight years later. Though Sozzi's 1957 critical edition is the basis for the Italian text and our translation, we have made some emendations for modern usage for a twenty-first century, English-speaking audience.

Additionally, only the first- and fifth-act choruses were part of the first performance in 1573. Two of the other choruses were originally separate poems, but all three of the other choruses seem to have been added by Tasso himself. There are *intermedii* between the acts, which include brief song poems accompanying music and dancing. (We would call them entr'actes or interludes today.) Whether they were written by Tasso for *Aminta* is a matter of some critical controversy, and modern editions in Italian and other languages sometimes include them, sometimes not. Because they seem integral to the meaning of the play, we have chosen to include them and to translate them. There is also a lengthy epilogue spoken by Venus, sometimes known under the title "Amor fuggitivo" or "Fleeting Love," in which Venus comes searching for her son Cupid, who has spoken the Prologue. It is not generally considered to be an authentic part of *Aminta,* however, and we have not included it here.

— Charles Jernigan and
Irene Marchegiani Jones

Biographical Chronology

1544 March 11. Torquato Tasso is born in Sorrento. His mother, Porzia de' Rossi, was from a Neapolitan noble family and his father, Bernando Tasso, a poet and intellectual, was at the court of Prince Ferrante Sanseverino. For political reasons, in 1552 Bernando is forced to move first to Rome and then to Urbino. Torquato follows his father.

1556 Torquato joins his father in Urbino and begins to study at the court of the Duke Guidobaldo II della Rovere. Among his instructors and mentors are Girolamo Muzio and Antonio Galli.

1559 He follows his father to Venice.

1560 He moves to Padua to study jurisprudence and later philosophy and rethoric. In Padua he meets Sperone Speroni and begins to explore the question of classical poetics.

1562 His first poem, *Rinaldo,* is published, and he writes love poetry for Lucrezia Bendidio and Laura Peperara.

1565 He is hired to work for Cardinal Luigi d'Este in Ferrara. Here he lives a few happy years as a respected and admired poet, before beginning a long period of suffering and distress.

1572 He begins to work for Duke Alfonso II, receiving as a courtier a considerable stipend for that time, which gives him the opportunity to dedicate himself to study and writing.

1573 In July, *Aminta* is performed for the first time.

1575 He finishes the poem *Goffredo,* later titled *Gerusalemme liberata (Jerusalem Delivered)* and published in 1581.
He becomes the court historian. This same year, doubts, hesitancies, and religious and moral problems start to trouble the poet, who becomes increasingly impatient and unhappy with court life.

1576 He composes *Allegoria della Liberata,* trying to justify the poem by explaining its concealed allegorical meaning.

1579 After a few years of ceaseless wandering and living in Rome, Sorrento, Venice, and Mantua, he comes back to Ferrara, always looking for the confirmation of people's admiration, respect for his literary glory, and a solution to his religious doubts. His restlessness and dissatisfaction with the court and himself bring the poet to inveigh against the duke and his family during Alfonso's marriage ceremony to Margherita Gongaza. He is arrested and held prisoner in Sant'Anna Hospital as a mentally unbalanced man for seven years. The motif for Alfonso's harsh treatment can be found in political and religious reasons rather than in the poet's real or imagined madness. His imprisonment, very harsh and strict at the beginning, is alleviated with time, and later the poet has permission to receive his friends' visits and go out, although accompanied. During these seven years, he alternates periods of relative tranquillity with periods of hallucinations and nightmares. He composes the *Dialogues* and an *Apologia* in defense of his major poem.

1586 He is allowed to leave the hospital and moves to Mantua where he is welcomed with respect and praise.

1587 He completes the tragedy *Torrismondo* and starts again to wander from one city to another, mostly residing in Rome and Naples.

1588 In Naples he begins to write the poem *Il Monte Oliveto,* in honor of the monastery where he is staying, and completes *The Life of St. Benedict.*

1592 He begins the religious poem entitled *Seven Days of Creation of the World.*

1593 He writes *Tears of the Virgin Mary* and *Tears of Jesus Christ.* He also completes the major revision of *Jerusalem Delivered,* which is published under the title of *Gerusalemme conquistata (Jerusalem Conquered).*

1594 As a result of a growing public recognition, the pope offers Tasso a stipend, promising to present him with the laurel crown on the Campidoglio.

1595 In March the poet becomes ill and dies on April 25.

Selected Bibliography

Accorsi, M. G. *Aminta: Ritorno a Saturno.* Soveria Mannelli (Catanzaro): Rubbettino, 1998.

—. *Pastori e teatro: Poesia e critica in Arcadia.* Modena: Mucchi, 1999.

Ariani, M., ed. *Il teatro italiano.* Vol. 2. Torino: Einaudi, 1977.

Barberi Squarotti, G. *Fine dell'idillio: Da Dante a Marino.* Genova: Il Melangolo, 1978.

Barberi Squarotti, G. "Il 'Far Grande' del Guarini." *Critica Letteraria* 22.3 (1994): 419–43.

Bauer R. et al. *The Renaissance Court: Sacred Space and Profane Hedonism.* 5 vols. Munich: Iudicium, 1990.

Bosco, U. "Medietà dell'*Aminta.*" *Saggi sul Rinascimento italiano.* Firenze: Le Monnier, 1970.

Brand, C. P. *Torquato Tasso. A Study of the Poet and of His Contribution to English Literature.* Cambridge: Cambridge University Press, 1965.

Buzzoni, A., ed. *Torquato Tasso fra letteratura, musica, teatro e arti figurative.* Bologna: Nuova Alfa, 1985.

Caretti, L. *Ariosto e Tasso.* Torino: Einaudi, 1961.

—. *Studi sulle rime del Tasso.* Roma: Ed. di Storia e Letteratura, 1950.

Chiodo, D. "Il mito dell'età aurea nell'opera tassiana." *Studi tassiani* 35 (1987): 31–58.

Cody, R. *The Landscape of the Mind: Pastoralism and Platonic Theory in Tasso's* Aminta *and Shakespeare's Early Comedies.* Oxford: Clarendon, 1969.

Daniele, A. *Nuovi capitoli tassiani.* Padova: Antenore, 1998.

Da Pozzo, G. *L'ambigua armonia: Studio sull'*Aminta *del Tasso.* Firenze: Olschki, 1983.

Da Pozzo, G., ed. *La Ragione e l'arte: Torquato Tasso e la Repubblica Veneta.* Venezia: Il Cardo, 1995.

De Robertis, G. "La fortuna dell'*Aminta.*" *Studi.* Florence: Le Monnier, 1944.

Della Terza, D. "La corte e il teatro: Il mondo del Tasso." *Il teatro italiano del Rinascimento.* Ed. M. De Panizza Lorch. Milano: Edizioni di Comunità, 1980, 51–63.

Donno, E., ed. *Three Renaissance Pastorals: Tasso–Guarini–Daniel.* Binghamton: Medieval and Renaissance Texts and Studies, 1993.

Entzminger, R. "The Politics of Love in Tasso's *Aminta* and Milton's *Comus.*" *Milton in Italy: Contexts, Images, Contradictions.* Ed. M. A. Di Cesare. Binghamton: Medieval and Renaissance Texts and Studies, 1991, 463–76.

Ferroni, G. *Il testo e la scena: Saggi sul teatro del Cinquecento.* Roma: Bulzoni, 1980.

—. "La scena, l'autore, il signore del teatro delle corti padane." *Il teatro italiano del Rinascimento.* Ed. M. de Panizza Lorch. Milano: Edizioni di Comunità, 1980.

Fubini, M. *Studi sulla letteratura del Rinascimento.* Firenze: La Nuova Italia, 1971.

Galli Stampino M. "The Rhetorical in Renaissance and Neoclassical Drama. Epideictic Pastoral: Rhetorical Tensions in Staging of Torquato Tasso's *Aminta.*" *Drama as Rhetoric/Rhetoric as Drama: An Exploration of Dramatic and Rhetorical Criticism.* Proceedings of a Conference at the University of South Carolina. 19–21 April, 1996. Tuscaloosa, AL: University of Alabama Press, 1997.

—. "Space of the Performance: *Aminta,* the Court, and the Theater." *Romance Review* 6.1 (1996): 7–28.

Getto, G. *Malinconia di Torquato Tasso.* 4th ed. Napoli: Liguori, 1986.

Jepson, L. "The *Aminta*: A Tragic Vision." *Rivista di Studi Italiani* 6.2 (1988): 23–34.

Klein, J. T. "Purloined Passages: Giraldi, Tasso and the Pastoral." *MLN* 99.1 (1984): 101–24.

Niccoli, G. A. *Cupid, Satyr, and the Golden Age: Pastoral Dramatic Scenes of the Late Renaissance.* New York: P. Lang, 1989.

Radcliff-Umstead, D. "Strutture del conflitto nel dramma pastorale tassiano." *Studi Tassiani* 24 (1974): 99–112.

Ramat, R. *Per la storia dello stile rinascimentale.* Messina – Firenze: D'Anna, 1953.

Romagnoli S. *Tasso.* Roma: G. Colombi, 1967.
Scrivano, R. "Tasso e il teatro." *La norma e lo scarto. Proposte per il Cinquecento letterario italiano.* Roma: Bonacci, 1980.
Shore, D. "The Shepherd and the Court: Pastoral Poetics in Spenser's *Colin Clout* and Tasso's *Aminta.*" *Canadian Review of Comparative Literature* 7.4 (1980): 394–410.
Sozzi, B. T. *Studi sul Tasso.* Pisa: Nistri Lischi, 1954.
—. "'Amor fuggitivo': Il cosiddetto epilogo dell' 'Aminta.'" *Bergomum: Bollettino della Civica Biblioteca* 80.3–4 (1985): 143–44.
Tasso, T. *Aminta.* Ed. C. Varese. Milano: Mursia, 1985.
—. *Aminta.* Ed. B. T. Sozzi. Padova: Liviana editrice, 1957.
—. *Poesie.* In *La letteratura italiana. Storia e testi.* Ed. F. Flora. Milano–Napoli: Riccardo Ricciardi, 1959.
Ulivi, F. *Il manierismo del Tasso e altri studi.* Firenze: Olschki, 1967.
Varese, C. *Torquato Tasso. Epos – Parola– Scena.* Messina–Firenze: D'Anna, 1976.
—. "Torquato Tasso." *I classici italiani nella storia della critica.* Ed. W. Binni. Firenze: La Nuova Italia, 1970.
—. *Quantitative History, Mannerism, and the Crisis of Aristocratic Hedonism.* New York: Garland, 1985.
Venturi, G., et al. *Torquato Tasso e la cultura estense.* Proceedings. of a Conference. Ferrara, 1995. Firenze: L. S. Olschki, 1999.
Zatti, S. "Natura e potere nell'Aminta." *Studi di filologia e letteratura offerti a Franco Croce.* Roma: Bulzoni, 1997.

Aminta

Favola Boschereccia

Aminta

A Pastoral Play

INTERLOCUTORI

Amore, in abito pastorale
Dafne, compagna di Silvia
Silvia, amata da Aminta
Aminta, innamorato di Silvia
Tirsi, compagno d'Aminta
Satiro, innamorato di Silvia
Nerina, messaggera
Ergasto, nunzio
Elpino, pastore
Coro de' pastori

SPEAKERS

Cupid, in pastoral dress, who speaks the Prologue
Dafne, a nymph, companion of Silvia
Silvia, a nymph in the service of Diana
Aminta, a shepherd in love with Silvia
Tirsi, a rustic poet, friend of Aminta
Elpino, a wise shepherd and poet
A Satyr, in love with Silvia
Nerina, a nymph
Ergasto, a messenger
Chorus of shepherds

Aminta

Prologo

Amore in abito pastorale

Amore

*Chi credería che sotto umane forme
e sotto queste pastorali spoglie
fosse nascosto un Dio? non mica un Dio
selvaggio, o de la plebe de gli dei,
ma tra' grandi e celesti il più potente,
che fa spesso cader di mano a Marte
la sanguinosa spada, ed a Nettuno
scotitor de la terra il gran tridente,
ed i folgori eterni al sommo Giove.
In questo aspetto, certo, e in questi panni
non riconoscerà sì di leggiero
Venere madre me suo figlio Amore.
Io da lei son constretto a fuggire
e celarmi da lei perch'ella vuole
ch'io di me stesso e de le mie saette
faccia a suo senno; e, qual femina, e quale
vana ed ambiziosa, mi respinge
pur tra le corti e tra corone e scettri,
e quivi vuole che impieghi ogni mia prova,
e solo al volgo de' ministri miei,
miei minori fratelli, ella consente
l'albergar tra le selve ed oprar l'armi
ne' rozzi petti. Io, che non son fanciullo,
se ben ho volto fanciullesco ed atti,
voglio dispor di me come a me piace;
ch'a me fu, non a lei, concessa in sorte
la face onnipotente, e l'arco d'oro.
Però spesso celandomi, e fuggendo*

Prologue

Prologue

Cupid, dressed as a shepherd

Cupid

Who would believe that clothed in human form
and so arrayed in shepherd's humble garb
a god could hide? And not a simple god
of country ways, of ordinary gods,
but greatest of the heavenly array,
who often from the hand of Mars strikes down
the bloody sword and from Neptune,
shaker of the earth, the great trident,
and lightening flashes from the great god Jove.
Even Mother — Venus — would not know
Cupid, me, her son, so easily
in this strange form, in these strange clothes.
It is from her I am constrained to fly
and hide myself because she always wants
to use both me and all my arrows just
as she desires; and she, that vain
ambitious woman, chases at my heels
in royal courts, among the crowns and scepters,
and there she would that I spend all my strength;
and only to the least among my aides,
my minor brothers, does she gives consent
to dwell within the woods and use their arms
on rustic breasts. While I, who am no child —
although a boy's face and acts are mine —
would like to live my life just as I please:
this since fate gave to me and not to her
the torch omnipotent and golden bow.
Thus often do I hide myself and flee,

l'imperio no, che in me non ha, ma i preghi,
c'han forza porti da importuna madre,
ricovero ne' boschi, e ne le case
de le genti minute; ella mi segue,
dar promettendo, a chi m'insegna a lei,
o dolci baci, o cosa altra più cara:
quasi io di dare in cambio non sia buono,
a chi mi tace, o mi nasconde a lei,
o dolci baci, o cosa altra più cara.
Questo io so certo almen: che i baci miei
saran sempre più cari a le fanciulle,
se io, che son l'Amor, d'amor m'intendo;
onde sovente ella mi cerca in vano,
che rivelarmi altri non vuole, e tace.
Ma per istarne anco più occulto, ond'ella
ritrovar non mi possa ai contrasegni,
deposto ho l'ali, la faretra e l'arco.
Non però disarmato io qui ne vengo,
che questa, che par verga, è la mia face
(così l'ho trasformata), e tutta spira
d'invisibili fiamme; e questo dardo,
se bene egli non ha la punta d'oro,
è di tempre divine, e imprime amore
dovunque fiede. Io voglio oggi con questo
far cupa e immedicabile ferita
nel duro sen de la più cruda ninfa
che mai seguisse il coro di Diana.
Né la piaga di Silvia fia minore
(che questo è 'l nome de l'alpestre ninfa)
che fosse quella che pur feci io stesso
nel molle sen d'Aminta, or son molt'anni,
quando lei tenerella ei tenerello
seguiva ne le caccie e ne i diporti.

not from her power, which has no force with me,
but from a mother's badgering, which has
its sway; I flee into the woods and homes
of common folk. And still she follows me,
and promises to all who tell of me
sweet kisses — or another thing more dear;
as if I could not give to those who keep
my secret or who hide me in exchange
sweet kisses or another thing more dear:
this much at least I know for sure, a kiss
of mine is always dearer to young girls,
if I, who am Love's self, love understand;
thus often she would search me out in vain,
for others won't reveal me and are quiet.
To make myself more difficult to find,
I've left behind my quiver, bow, and wings,
so she could never find me by those signs.
Don't think however that I come disarmed,
for this, which seems a rod, is my great torch
(I've changed it into this), and it breathes forth
a flame invisible; so too this dart,
which though it lacks the famous golden point,
was tempered by the gods and forges love
where'er it strikes. With it today I'd like
to make a wound that's deep, that can't be healed,
deep in the breast of that most cruel nymph
who ever followed in Diana's train.
Nor may the wound of Silvia be less
(for that's the name of this wild mountain nymph)
than that grave wound that once I made myself
within Aminta's breast, now years ago,
when she, a fair young maid, and he a lad,
took part together in the hunt and games.

*E, perché il colpo mio più in lei s'interni,
aspetterò che la pietà mollisca
quel duro gelo che d'intorno al core
l'ha ristretto il rigor de l'onestate
e del virginal fasto; ed in quel punto
ch'ei fia più molle, lancerogli il dardo.
E, per far sì bell'opra a mio grand'agio,
io ne vo a mescolarmi infra la turba
de' pastori festanti e coronati,
che già qui s'è inviata, ove a diporto
si sta ne' dì solenni, esser fingendo
uno di loro schiera: e in questo luogo,
in questo luogo a punto io farò il colpo,
che veder non potrallo occhio mortale.
Queste selve oggi ragionar d'Amore
s'udranno in nuova guisa: e ben parassi
che la mia deità sia qui presente
in se medesima, e non ne' suoi ministri.
Spirerò nobil sensi a' rozzi petti,
raddolcirò de le lor lingue il suono;
perché, ovunque i' mi sia, io sono Amore,
ne' pastori non men che ne gli eroi,
e la disagguaglianza de' soggetti
come a me piace agguaglio' e questa è pure
suprema gloria e gran miracol mio:
render simili a le più dotte cetre
le rustiche sampogne; e, se mia madre,
che si sdegna vedermi errar fra' boschi,
ciò non conosce, è cieca ella, e non io,
cui cieco a torto il cieco volgo appella.*

And that my blow may penetrate still more
in her, I'll wait till pity's grief will melt
the icy grip that holds about her heart
and long has kept her chaste and pure, a virgin,
disdainful of all love; and in that point
where it is softest, there I'll launch my dart.[1]
To bring about such good works at my ease,
I go forth, mixing with the common crowd
of festive shepherds crowned and garlanded,
who go to where amusement is on days
of high festivity; I feign to be
one of their band, and it is in this place,
this very place, that I will strike the blow,
but mortal's eye will never see it fly.
These forest paths will hear Love spoken of
in all new ways; and then it will appear
that my godhead is present in this place,
itself and not in ministers and aides.
Nobly inspired shall be these rustic breasts,
and I shall sweeten so their songs' rough sounds
for I am Love wherever I may be,
not less among the shepherds than the great,
and inequality of those I rule,
if I desire, I equalize. And this
is my great miracle and glory supreme,
to make the rustic bagpipe equal to
the cultivated lyre. If mother, who
disdains to see me wander in the woods,
does not know that, then she is blind, not I,
whom, wrongly, blind and vulgar folk call "blind."

Aminta

Atto Primo

Scena Prima
Dafne, Silvia

Dafne

Vorrai dunque pur, Silvia,
dai piaceri di Venere lontana
menarne tu questa tua giovanezza?
Né 'l dolce nome di madre udirai,
né intorno ti vedrai vezzosamente
scherzar i figli pargoletti? Ah, cangia,
cangia, prego, consiglio,
pazzarella che sei.

Silvia

Altri segua i diletti de l'amore,
(se pur v'è ne l'amor alcun diletto):
me questa vita giova, e 'l mio trastullo
è la cura de l'arco e degli strali;
seguir le fere fugaci, e le forti
atterrar combattendo; e, se non mancano
saette a la faretra, o fere al bosco,
non tem'io che a me manchino diporti.

Dafne

Insipidi diporti veramente,
ed insipida vita: e, s'a te piace,
è sol perché non hai provata l'altra.
Così la gente prima, che già visse
nel mondo ancora semplice ed infante,
stimò dolce bevanda e dolce cibo
l'acqua e le ghiande, ed or l'acqua e le ghiande

Act One

Scene One
Dafne and Silvia

Dafne

You would, then, really, Silvia,
waste all the passing youthful years
far from the pleasures Venus offers us?
Nor would you hear the sweet name "mother" sound,
nor see around you, laughing joyously,
your little children playing? Change, ah, change,
I counsel you, I pray
you rash and foolish girl.

Silvia

Let others follow after love's delights,
if there is really some delight in love:
for me this life is good; and my delight
lies in the use of bow and of the shafts,
and in the chase of beasts, and striking down
the strong to earth; and if the beasts still roam
the wood and if my quiver's full,
then I'll not fear a lack of happy times.

Dafne

Such little-pleasant pleasures truly they,
such little-pleasant life; if it seems sweet,
it's just because you have not tried my way.
Thus once the folk who first inhabited
the earth when it was young and simple still
held water as sweet drink and acorns as
sweet food; and acorns now and water, both,

sono cibo e bevanda d'animali,
poi che s'è posto in uso il grano e l'uva.
Forse, se tu gustassi anco una volta
la millesima parte de le gioie
che gusta un cor amato riamando,
diresti, ripentita, sospirando:
perduto è tutto il tempo
che in amar non si spende.
O mia fuggita etate,
quante vedove notti,
quanti dì solitari
ho consumati indarno,
che impiegar si poteano in quest'uso,
il qual più replicato è più soave!
Cangia, cangia consiglio,
pazzarella che sei:
che 'l pentirsi da sezzo nulla giova.

SILVIA

Quando io dirò, pentita, sospirando,
queste parole che tu fingi ed orni
come a te piace, torneranno i fiumi
a le lor fonti, e i lupi fuggiranno
dagli agni, e 'l veltro le timide lepri,
amerà l'orso il mare, e 'l delfin l'alpi.

DAFNE

Conosco la ritrosa fanciullezza:
qual tu sei, tal io fui: così portava
la vita e 'l volto, e così biondo il crine,
e così vermigliuzza avea la bocca,
e così mista col candor la rosa
ne le guancie pienotte e delicate.

are only food and drink for forest beasts,
since now we use the fruit of grain and grape.
Perhaps if only once you did enjoy
the thousandth part of all the happiness
a heart beloved enjoys, returning love,
repentant, you would surely sighing say,
"All time is truly lost and gone
which is not spent in serving love."
Oh, fled are all my youthful years,
how many widowed nights I've watched,
how many solitary days
I've wasted, wasted all in vain,
which could be spent in loving, being loved —
which sweeter still becomes the more it's done!
Change, oh change I counsel you,
you rash and foolish girl:
regret when one is old's not worth a jot.

SILVIA

When I shall speak, all penitent and sighing,
these words you feign, these words you ornament
as pleases you, the rivers will return
to springs that are their source, the wolves will flee
from sheep, and from the timid hare, the hound;
the bear will love the sea, the dolphin, peaks.[2]

DAFNE

I understand your bashful girlishness:
what you are, so was I; like you I led
my careless life, like you I had blond locks,
like you my lips wore a vermilion hue,
like you the red rose and white were mixed
within my cheeks, both delicate and full.

*Era il mio sommo gusto (or me n'avveggio,
gusto di sciocca) sol tender le reti,
ed invescar le panie, ed aguzzare
il dardo ad una cote, e spiar l'orme
e 'l covil de le fere: e, se talora
vedea guatarmi da cupido amante,
chinava gli occhi rustica e selvaggia,
piena di sdegno e di vergogna, e m'era
mal grata la mia grazia, e dispiacente
quanto di me piaceva altrui: pur come
fosse mia colpa e mia onta e mio scorno
l'esser guardata, amata e desiata.
Ma che non puote il tempo? e che non puote,
servendo, meritando, supplicando,
fare un fedele ed importuno amante?
Fui vinta, io te 'l confesso, e furon l'armi
del vincitore umiltà, sofferenza,
pianti, sospiri, e dimandar mercede.
Mostrommi l'ombra d'una breve notte
allora quel che 'l lungo corso e 'l lume
di mille giorni non m'avea mostrato;
ripresi allor me stessa e la mia cieca
simplicitate, e dissi sospirando:
"Eccoti, Cinzia, il corno, eccoti l'arco,
ch'io rinunzio i tuoi strali e la tua vita."
Così spero veder ch'anco il tuo Aminta
pur un giorno domestichi la tua
rozza selvatichezza, ed ammollisca
questo tuo cor di ferro e di macigno.
Forse ch'ei non è bello? o ch'ei non t'ama?
o ch'altri lui non ama? o ch'ei si cambia
per l'amor d'altri? over per l'odio tuo?
forse ch'in gentilezza egli ti cede?*

It was my greatest joy (and now I know
a foolish joy indeed) to spread the nets
and set the snares to trap and sharpen all
the arrowheads upon the stone and spy
the prints and lairs of beasts; and if perchance
I saw a lustful man admiring me,
I lowered my eyes, and I was rustic, wild,
full of disdain and shame; to me myself
my beauty was not beautiful, and I
disdained what pleased another's eyes in me:
how great I felt my guilt, my shame, my scorn
to be admired and loved, to be desired.
But what can time not do? And what will not
avail a faithful man who makes his point
by serving, pleading, meriting my love?
So I was conquered, I confess; the arms
he bore were patience, tears, humility,
and sighs, and pleading for my mercy's gift.
Within the dark'ning space of one short night
he showed me more than all the brilliant light
of days and days — a thousand — ever showed.
Then I reproved myself and all my blind
simplicity, and I said, sighing still:
"Here, Cynthia,[3] your horn, and here your bow,
for I renounce your arrows and your ways."
It's thus I hope one day to see that your
Aminta still shall civilize your wild
and wooden ways and thus will soften so
your heart, as hard as iron and rocky stone.
Perhaps he's ugly? Or he loves you not?
Or does he love another? Or he's changed
since others love him, or for hating you?
And is he of less gentle birth than you?

Se tu sei figlia di Cidippe, a cui
fu padre il Dio di questo nobil fiume,
ed egli è figlio di Silvano, a cui
Pane fu padre, il gran Dio de' pastori.
Non è men di te bella, se ti guardi
dentro lo specchio mai d'alcuna fonte,
la candida Amarilli; e pur ei sprezza
le sue dolci lusinghe, e segue i tuoi
dispettosi fastidi. Or fingi (e voglia
pur Dio che questo fingere sia vano)
ch'egli, teco sdegnato, al fin procuri
ch'a lui piaccia colei cui tanto ei piace:
qual animo fia il tuo? o con quali occhi
il vedrai fatto altrui? fatto felice
ne l'altrui braccia, e te schernir ridendo?

SILVIA

Faccia Aminta di sé e de' suoi amori
quel ch'a lui piace: a me nulla ne cale;
e, pur che non sia mio, sia di chi vuole;
ma esser non può mio s'io lui non voglio;
né, s'anco egli mio fosse, io sarei sua.

DAFNE

Onde nasce il tuo odio?

SILVIA

Dal suo amore.

DAFNE

Piacevol padre di figlio crudele.
Ma quando mai dai mansueti agnelli
nacquer le tigri? o dai bei cigni i corvi?
O me inganni, o te stessa.

If you are daughter to Cidippe, whose
own father was the noble river's god,[4]
then he is son of Silvanus, to whom
great Pan was sire, the shepherd's noble god.[5]
No lovely less than you, if you should glance
within the mirror of some fountain's pond,
is lovely Amaryllis; and yet he
disdains her sweet attraction, following
your scornful ways. So let's pretend (and pray
to God that this is only vain pretense)
that he, disdaining you, should find in her
a girl who pleases him, by whom he's loved.
Then how would you react? And with what thoughts
will you see him within another's arms,
made happy there, and laughing, scorning you?

SILVIA

Whatever pleases him, Aminta can
do with himself and with his loves; I do
not care. Since I don't want him, let him be
whose love he would, for mine he cannot be,
and even were he mine, I'd not be his.

DAFNE

And what gave birth to such a hate?

SILVIA

His love.

DAFNE

A gentle father of a cruel child.
But when were tigers born of peaceful sheep?
Or when from lovely swans did crows come forth?
You fool yourself or me.

SILVIA

Odio il suo amore
ch'odia la mia onestate, ed amai lui
mentr'ei volse di me quel ch'io voleva.

DAFNE

Tu volevi il tuo peggio: egli a te brama
quel ch'a sé brama.

SILVIA

Dafne, o taci, o parla
d'altro, se vuoi risposta.

DAFNE

Or guata modi!
guata che dispettosa giovinetta!
Or rispondimi almen: s'altri t'amasse,
gradiresti il suo amore in questa guisa?

SILVIA

In questa guisa gradirei ciascuno
insidiator di mia virginitate,
che tu dimandi amante, ed io nimico.

DAFNE

Stimi dunque nemico
il monton de l'agnella?
de la giovenca il toro?
Stimi dunque nemico
il tortore a la fida tortorella?
Stimi dunque stagione
di nimicizia e d'ira
la dolce primavera,
ch'or allegra e ridente

SILVIA

I hate his love
who hates my chastity, and I loved him
when he desired the things that I desired.

DAFNE

What you want is less good: he wants for you
what he wants for himself.

SILVIA

Now Dafne, quiet,
if you want my replies.

DAFNE

Oh, see your ways!
See how dispiteous a girl she is!
Now answer this at least: if someone else
loved you, would you receive his love like this?

SILVIA

In this way would I welcome every man
who came to tempt my sweet virginity.
You call him lover; I, an enemy.

DAFNE

Do you believe the ram
is hateful to the ewe?
The cow disdains the bull?
Do you believe the dove
is hateful to the faithful turtledove?
Do you believe a time
of enmity and hate
the sweet seed-time of spring,
which now rejoices

riconsiglia ad amare
il mondo e gli animali
e gli uomini e le donne? e non t'accorgi
come tutte le cose
or sono innamorate
d'un amor pien di gioia e di salute?
Mira là quel colombo
con che dolce susurro lusingando
bacia la sua compagna.
Odi quell'usignuolo
che va di ramo in ramo
cantando: Io amo, io amo*; e, se no 'l sai,*
la biscia lascia il suo veleno e corre
cupida al suo amatore;
van le tigri in amore;
ama il leon superbo; e tu sol, fiera
più che tutte le fere,
albergo gli dineghi nel tuo petto.
Ma che dico leoni e tigri e serpi,
che pur han sentimento? amano ancora
gli alberi. Veder puoi con quanto affetto
e con quanti iterati abbracciamenti
la vite s'avviticchia al suo marito;
l'abete ama l'abete, il pino il pino,
l'orno per l'orno e per la salce il salce
e l'un per l'altro faggio arde e sospira.
Quella quercia, che pare
sì ruvida e selvaggia,
sent'anch'ella il potere
de l'amoroso foco; e, se tu avessi
spirto e senso d'amore, intenderesti
i suoi muti sospiri. Or tu da meno
esser vuoi de le piante,

and smiling, reconciles
the world and animals
and men and women all to love? And don't
you see how all the earth
is now infused with love,
a love that's good and full of joy and health?
See there that loving dove,
who softly calling, sweetly murmuring,
does kiss his loving mate;
Oh, hear that nightingale
who flies from limb to limb
and sings, *I love, I love*; and even snakes
let venom go and hurry on,
desirous, to their loves;
the tigers fall in love;
the proud lion loves; and you alone refuse,
more fierce than all the beasts,
to grant a place to him within your breast.
But did I say that serpents, tigers, lions
alone have love's sweet self? No, even trees
may love. How much affection you can see,
and with how many sweet embracing folds
the vine entwines about the one it loves;
the fir tree loves the fir, the pine, the pine,
the flowering ash, the ash, the willow loves
its own, and beech for beech will burn and sigh.
That oak, which may appear
so rough, so coarse, so wild,
feels, even it, the force
the loving fire exerts: and if you felt
or knew of love, then you would understand
its silent sighs. Now do you wish to be
less even than the plants,

per non esser amante?
Cangia, cangia consiglio,
pazzarella che sei.

SILVIA

Or su, quando i sospiri
udirò de le piante,
io son contenta allor d'esser amante.

DAFNE

Tu prendi a gabbo i miei fidi consigli
e burli mie ragioni? O in amore
sorda non men che sciocca! Ma va' pure,
che verrà tempo che ti pentirai
non averli seguiti. E già non dico
allor che fuggirai le fonti, ov'ora
spesso ti specchi e forse ti vagheggi,
allor che fuggirai le fonti, solo
per tema di vederti crespa e brutta;
questo avverratti ben; ma non t'annuncio
già questo solo, che, bench'è gran male,
è però mal commune. Or non rammenti
ciò che l'altr'ieri Elpino raccontava,
il saggio Elpino a la bella Licori,
Licori ch'in Elpin puote con gli occhi
qual ch'ei potere in lei dovria col canto,
se 'l dovere in amor si ritrovasse?
E 'l raccontava udendo Batto e Tirsi
gran maestri d'amore, e 'l raccontava
ne l'antro de l'Aurora, ove su l'uscio
è scritto: Lungi, ah lungi ite, profani.
Diceva egli, e diceva che glie 'l disse
quel grande che cantò l'armi e gli amori,

so not to be in love?
Change, oh, change I counsel you,
you rash and foolish girl.

SILVIA

Well, when I hear the sighs
escape the plants that woo,
then I'll be glad to be a lover too.

DAFNE

You take my faithful counsels all as jest,
deride my thoughts, though one who's deaf to love
is sure the fool! But go your way, for soon
a time will come when you will sore repent
not having followed them. And then I know
that you will flee the fountains where you now
can see your image proudly gazing back,
then you shall flee the fountains, all alone,
afraid to see yourself all wrinkled, gray:
this is the truth; but I'm not telling you
just this, for though it is an ill that's great,
it is the common ill. Do you recall
what just the other day Elpino said,
Elpin' the wise to lovely Licori,[6]
she who could stir Elpino with her eyes
as he should have such power with her through song,
if words like "should" were ever found in love?
He told her in the grotto of Aurora,[7]
upon whose door is writ, *Stay out, profane,*
what Tirsi once with Batto spoke about —
they know of love — and this is what he said[8]:
he told of all that he had heard and learned
from that great man who sang of arms and loves,

ch'a lui lasciò la fistola morendo,
che là giù ne lo 'nferno è un nero speco,
là dove essala un fumo pien di puzza
da le triste fornaci d'Acheronte;
e che quivi punite eternamente
in tormenti di tenebre e di pianto
son le femine ingrate e sconoscenti.
Quivi aspetta ch'albergo s'apparecchi
a la tua feritate;
e dritto è ben ch'il fumo
tragga mai sempre il pianto da quegli occhi
onde trarlo giamai
non poté la pietate.
Segui, segui tuo stile,
ostinata che sei.

SILVIA

Ma che fe' allor Licori? e com' rispose
a queste cose?

DAFNE

Tu de' fatti propri
nulla ti curi, e vuoi saper gli altrui.
Con gli occhi gli rispose.

SIVLIA

Come risponder sol poté con gli occhi?

DAFNE

Risposer questi con dolce sorriso,
volti ad Elpino: "Il core e noi siam tuoi;
tu bramar più non déi: costei non puote
più darti." E tanto solo basterebbe
per intiera mercede al casto amante,

who, dying, left to him his shepherd's pipes:
that down within the pit of hell a cave
lies, black, and there exhales a smoky stench
from Acheron's sad furnaces spewed forth,
and there it is that in eternal pain,
tormented by the darkness and by tears,
are punished thankless and ungrateful girls.[9]
There they prepare a place awaiting you —
which fits your fierce, wild ways —
and it is right that there
the smoke draws ever from those eyes sad tears,
where pity never could
draw forth a single tear.
So go on down your road,
stubborn as you are.

SILVIA

But how did Licori behave, and what
did she reply?

DAFNE

You would ignore the facts
that matter, and then turn to other things.
She answered with her eyes.

SILVIA

How could she answer with her eyes alone?

DAFNE

Her eyes so sweetly smiling seemed to speak,
turned towards Elpin' — "My heart and I are yours;
you must desire no more, for we cannot
give more to you." And that would be enough
for recompense from such a pure love

se stimasse veraci come belli
quegli occhi, e lor prestasse intera fede.

SILVIA

E perché lor non crede?

DAFNE

Or tu non sai
ciò che Tirsi ne scrisse, allor ch'ardendo
forsennato egli errò per le foreste,
sì ch'insieme movea pietate e riso
ne le vezzose ninfe e ne' pastori?
Né già cose scrivea degne di riso,
se ben cose facea degne di riso.
Lo scrisse in mille piante, e con le piante
crebbero i versi; e così lessi in una:
Specchi del cor, fallaci infidi lumi,
ben riconosco in voi gli inganni vostri:
ma che pro, se schivarli Amor mi toglie?

SILVIA

Io qui trapasso il tempo ragionando,
né mi sovvien ch'oggi è 'l dì prescritto
ch'andar si deve a la caccia ordinata
ne l'Eliceto. Or, se ti pare, aspetta
ch'io pria deponga nel solito fonte
il sudore e la polve ond'ier mi sparsi
seguendo in caccia una damma veloce
ch'al fin giunsi ed ancisi.

DAFNE

Aspetterotti,
e forse anch'io mi bagnerò nel fonte.

if he had thought those eyes as truthful as
they lovely were, and given them his faith.

SILVIA

Why didn't he believe?

DAFNE

Now don't you know
what Tirsi wrote about when full of love
he wandered like a madman through the woods,
so that the gracious nymphs and shepherds there
were moved to pity and to laugh at once?
And although he wrote nothing laughable,
the things he did were truly laughable.
He wrote it on a thousand trees, that verse
and tree would grow as one; and I thus read:
You mirrors of the heart, unfaithful eyes,
how well I recognize in you deceit:
and yet for what, if Love allows no flight?[10]

SILVIA

I waste my time in speaking here with you,
and I'd forgot today's the day prescribed
for me to join the hunt that's been prepared
there in the ilex grove.[11] Wait if you like
while I go bathe down at the spring to wash
the sweat and dust, which clings since yesterday
when chasing in the hunt a speeding deer
I caught and struck it down.

DAFNE

I shall await
you and perhaps I'll bathe too in the spring.

Ma sino a le mie case ir prima voglio,
che l'ora non è tarda, come pare.
Tu ne le tue m'aspetta ch'a te venga
e pensa in tanto pur quel che più importa
de la caccia e del fonte; e, se non sai,
credi di non saper, e credi a' savi.

Scena Seconda
Aminta, Tirsi

AMINTA

Ho visto al pianto mio
risponder per pietate i sassi e l'onde,
e sospirar le fronde
ho visto al pianto mio;
ma non ho visto mai,
né spero di vedere,
compassion ne la crudele e bella
che non so s'io mi chiami o donna o fera:
ma niega d'esser donna,
poiché nega pietate
a chi non la negaro
le cose inanimate.

TIRSI

Pasce l'agna l'erbette, il lupo l'agne,
ma il crudo Amor di lagrime si pasce,
né se ne mostra mai satollo.

AMINTA

Ahi, lasso,
ch'Amor satollo è del mio pianto omai,

But first I want to go back home again
because it's not as late as it may seem.
You wait in your abode until I come
and think meanwhile of that which matters more
than either hunt or bath: if you know not,
admit your ignorance and trust the wise.

Scene Two
Aminta and Tirsi

Aminta

Unto my tears I've seen
the rocks and waves for pity's sake reply,
and leaves all seem to sigh
unto my tears I've seen;
but I have never seen,
nor ever hope to see
compassion in the one who's cruel and fair,
though if she's beast or woman, I know not:
but she denies her womanhood
since pity she denies
to one who's even pitied
by things inanimate.

Tirsi

The sheep will feed on grass, the wolf on sheep,
but Love, who's cruel, will feed upon our tears,
and he is never satisfied.

Aminta

Alas!
May Love be gorged upon my tears at last,

e solo ha sete del mio sangue, e tosto
voglio ch'egli e quest'empia il sangue mio
bevan con gli occhi.

TIRSI

Ahi, Aminta, ahi, Aminta,
che parli? o che vaneggi? Or ti conforta,
ch'un'altra troverai, se ti disprezza
questa crudele.

AMINTA

Ohimè, come poss'io
altri trovar, se me trovar non posso?
Se perduto ho me stesso, quale acquisto
farò mai che mi piaccia?

TIRSI

O miserello,
non disperar, ch'acquisterai costei.
La lunga etate insegna a l'uom di porre
freno a i leoni ed a le tigri ircane.

AMINTA

Ma il misero non puote a la sua morte
indugio sostener di lungo tempo.

TIRSI

Sarà corto l'indugio: in breve spazio
s'adira e in breve spazio anco si placa
femina, cosa mobil per natura
più che fraschetta al vento e più che cima
di pieghevole spica. Ma, ti prego,
fa ch'io sappia più a dentro de la tua

and only want my blood; and then I wish
that he and she who has no pity, both
would drink it with their eyes.

TIRSI

Aminta, ah,
what say you? What wild words. Be comforted,
you'll find another girl if one so cruel
despises you.

AMINTA

Alas! How can I find
another if I cannot find myself?
If I have lost myself what new conquest
that pleases me could I make now?

TIRSI

Poor man,
do not despair, for you will find her soon.
In time a man can learn to civilize
the lions and tigers of Ircania.[12]

AMINTA

But one who's miserable cannot sustain
for very long postponement of his death.

TIRSI

Your waiting will be short: in little time
a woman takes offense and then forgives
in little time; by nature whimsical,
twigs scattered by the blowing wind, worse than
the supple corn stalk's top. But let me know,
I pray, still more about your grief and hard

dura condizione e de l'amore;
che se ben confessato m'hai più volte
d'amare, mi tacesti però dove
fosse posto l'amore. Ed è ben degna
la fedele amicizia ed il commune
studio de le Muse ch'a me scuopra
ciò ch'a gli altri si cela.

AMINTA

Io son contento,
Tirsi, a te dir ciò che le selve e i monti
e i fiumi sanno, e gli uomini non sanno.
Ch'io sono ormai sì prossimo a la morte,
ch'è ben ragion ch'io lasci chi ridica
la cagion del morire, e che l'incida
ne la scorza d'un faggio, presso il luogo
dove sarà sepolto il corpo essangue;
sì che talor passandovi quell'empia
si goda di calcar l'ossa infelici
co 'l piè superbo, e tra sé dica: "È questo
pur mio trionfo"; e goda di vedere
che nota sia la sua vittoria a tutti
li pastor paesani e pellegrini
che quivi il caso guidi; e forse (ahi, spero
troppo alte cose) un giorno esser potrebbe
ch'ella, commossa da tarda pietate,
piangesse morto chi già vivo uccise,
dicendo: "Oh pur qui fosse, e fosse mio!"
Or odi.

TIRSI

Segui pur, ch'io ben t'ascolto,
e forse a miglior fin che tu non pensi.

condition and about your love within:
if often you've confessed to me of love,
you are, however, silent on just where
your love is placed; and it is worthy of
a faithful friendship and our joint pursuit
to find our Muse[13] that you should let me know
what you have hid from others.

AMINTA

I am glad
to tell you, Tirsi, what the beasts and hills
and rivers know, but what no man perceives:
that I am now so intimate with death
that it is right that I should tell someone
who can rehearse the reason that I died
and carve upon some beech's bark, nearby
the place my lifeless corpse shall buried be,
so that she, pitiless, when passing there,
shall gladden, trampling my unhappy bones
with her proud foot, and to herself shall say:
"This is my victory," exulting that
her victory is known to all of those —
the peasant shepherds and the pilgrims who
are guided there by chance. And just perhaps
(I hope, ah, for too much) one day she'll come,
and touched by pity felt too late, then she
might mourn a dead man whom, alive, she killed,
and say: "Oh, were he here and were he mine!"
Now hear.

TIRSI

Go on, for I am listening well,
perhaps to better purpose than you think.

AMINTA

Essendo io fanciulletto, sì che a pena
giunger potea con la man pargoletta
a côrre i frutti dai piegati rami
degli arboscelli, intrinseco divenni
de la più vaga e cara verginella
che mai spiegasse al vento chioma d'oro.
La figliuola conosci di Cidippe
e di Montan, ricchissimo d'armenti,
Silvia, onor de le selve, ardor de l'alme?
Di questa parlo, ahi lasso; vissi a questa
così unito alcun tempo, che fra due
tortorelle più fida compagnia
non sarà mai, né fue.
Congiunti eran gli alberghi,
ma più congiunti i cori;
conforme era l'etate,
ma 'l pensier più conforme;
seco tendeva insidie con le reti
ai pesci ed agli augelli, e seguitava
i cervi seco e le veloci damme:
e 'l diletto e la preda era commune.
Ma, mentre io fea rapina d'animali,
fui non so come a me stesso rapito.
A poco a poco nacque nel mio petto,
non so da qual radice,
com'erba suol che per se stessa germini,
un incognito affetto
che mi fea desiare
d'esser sempre presente
a la mia bella Silvia;
e bevea da' suoi lumi
un'estranea dolcezza,

Act One, Scene Two

AMINTA

Once when a little lad, so young I scarce
could reach with childish hand to take the fruit
that hung down off the laden branches of
sweet smelling trees, then I became the friend
of one who was the loveliest dear maid
whose golden hair e'er spread out on the wind.
Do you know her — Cidippe's daughter, child
of rich Montanus, he most rich in herds —
the forest's honor, Silvia, the warmth
of hearts? I speak of her, alas! I lived
a time united to her so that two
sweet turtledoves were never nor shall be
such faithful friends as we.
Our homes were joined as one,
our hearts were closer still;
our age was consonant,
more consonant our thoughts.
With her I laid the traps and spread the nets
to catch the fish and birds and joined the chase
with her to catch the stags and speeding deer:
the pleasure and the prey our common joy.
But while I chased the animals for prey,
I don't know how, but I fell prey myself.
And bit by bit was born within my breast,
I don't know from what root,
as grass may seem to germinate itself,
a strange affection that
made me desire to be
forever present where
my lovely Silvia was.
I drank from her soft eyes
a newfound sweetness, one

che lasciava nel fine
un nonso che d'amaro;
sospirava sovente, e non sapeva
la cagion de' sospiri.
Così fui prima amante ch'intendessi
che cosa fosse Amore.
Ben me n'accorsi al fin: ed in qual modo,
ora m'ascolta, e nota.

TIRSI

È da notare.

AMINTA

A l'ombra d'un bel faggio Silvia e Filli
sedean un giorno, ed io con loro insieme,
quando un'ape ingegnosa, che cogliendo
sen' giva il mel per que' prati fioriti,
a le guancie di Fillide volando,
a le guancie vermiglie come rosa,
le morse e le rimorse avidamente:
ch'a la similitudine ingannata
forse un fior le credette. Allora Filli
cominciò lamentarsi, impaziente
de l'acuta puntura:
ma la mia bella Silvia disse: "Taci,
taci, non ti lagnar, Filli, perch'io
con parole d'incanti leverotti
il dolor de la picciola ferita.
A me insegnò già questo secreto
la saggia Aresia, e n'ebbe per mercede
quel mio corno d'avolio ornato d'oro.
Così dicendo, avvicinò le labra
de la sua bella e dolcissima bocca

that left a bitter taste
somehow, I don't know why:
so soft I often sighed and scarce I knew
the reasons why I sighed.
And thus I was a lover e'er I knew
a single thing of love.
And so I've finally come to this, and in
what way, now hear and closely note.

TIRSI

Go on.

AMINTA

Beneath a beech's silvery shade one day
did Silvia and Filli sit with me
when through the flowering fields a bee did fly
industr'ous at its task of gathering sweet,
and flying, it rose up to Filli's cheeks,
her cheeks vermilion as the rose is red,
and avidly it bit her, bit again:
fooled by the close similitude perhaps,
it thought she was a flower. Filli then
began to cry and fretfully lament
the sharpness of the wound;
but then my lovely Silvia said, "Be quiet,
be quiet, O Filli, don't lament, because
with words of incantation I can raise
the pain that's caused you by the little wound.
The wise Aresia taught me once the words,
a secret, and she had as thanks from me
my ivory hunting horn, adorned with gold."
So saying, she then brought up close the lips
of that so sweet and, oh, so lovely mouth

a la guancia rimorsa, e con soave
sussurro mormorò non so che versi.
Oh mirabili effetti! Sentì tosto
cessar la doglia, o fosse la virtute
di que' magici detti, o, com'io credo,
la virtù de la bocca
che sana ciò che tocca.
Io, che sino a quel punto altro non volsi
che 'l soave splendor degli occhi belli,
e le dolci parole, assai più dolci
che 'l mormorar d'un lento fiumicello
che rompa il corso fra minuti sassi
o che 'l garrir de l'aura infra le frondi,
allor sentii nel cor novo desire
d'appressare a la sua questa mia bocca;
e fatto non so come astuto e scaltro
più de l'usato (guarda quanto Amore
aguzza l'intelletto!) mi sovvenne
d'un inganno gentile co 'l qual io
recar potessi a fine il mio talento;
che fingendo ch'un'ape avesse morso
il mio labbro di sotto, incominciai
a lamentarmi di cotal maniera
che quella medicina che la lingua
non richiedeva, il volto richiedeva.
La semplicetta Silvia,
pietosa del mio male,
s'offrì di dar aita
a la finta ferita, ahi lasso, e fece
più cupa e più mortale
la mia piaga verace,
quando le labra sue
giunse a le labra mie.

near to the bitten cheek, and with such soft,
smooth whispers murmured low I know not what.
Oh, marvelous effects! Immediately
the pain grew still: were it the power of
those magic words, or, as I do believe,
the power of her lips,
which cures with a kiss.
I, who only wished 'til then to see
the soft illumination of her eyes,
to hear the sweetness of her words, more sweet
than is the murmur of the gentle stream
that runs its course among the little stones,
or sweeter than the breeze among the leaves,
oh, it was then I felt a new desire
within my heart, to bring my mouth to hers
and made, I don't know how, astute and sly —
more than I'd been before (see how much Love
can sharpen intellect!) — a gentle trick
did come to me with which I thought that I
could use my skill to gain the end I sought.
So feigning that a bee had bitten me
upon my lower lip, I did begin
to weep, lamenting so, in such a way
that her sweet remedy, which tongue could not
request, was thus requested by my face.
The simple Silvia
took pity on my ill
and offered to give aid
to my feigned wound, alas, and made for me
a real wound, deeper far,
more mortal than the false,
when her sweet lips rose up
and met these lips of mine.

Né l'api d'alcun fiore
còglion sì dolce il mel ch'allora io colsi
da quelle fresche rose,
se ben gli ardenti baci,
che spingeva il desire a inumidirsi,
raffrenò la temenza
e la vergogna, o felli
più lenti e meno audaci.
Ma mentre al cor scendeva
quella dolcezza mista
d'un secreto veleno,
tal diletto n'avea
che, fingendo ch'ancor non mi passasse
il dolor di quel morso,
fei sì ch'ella più volte
vi replicò l'incanto.
Da indi in qua andò in guisa crescendo
il desire e l'affanno impaziente
che, non potendo più capir nel petto,
fu forza che scoppiasse; ed una volta
che in cerchio sedevam ninfe e pastori
e facevamo alcuni nostri giuochi,
che ciascun ne l'orecchio del vicino
mormorando diceva un suo secreto,
"Silvia," le dissi, "io per te ardo, e certo
morrò se non m'aiti." A quel parlare
chinò ella il bel volto, e fuor le venne
un improvviso insolito rossore
che diede segno di vergogna e d'ira:
né ebbi altra risposta che un silenzio,
un silenzio turbato e pien di dure
minaccie. Indi si tolse, e più non volle
né vedermi né udirmi. E già tre volte

No bee did ever take
a nectar half so sweet as that I took
from her fresh, rose-like lips.
Although my ardent kisses
thrust up all my desire, bedewing it,
my dread and shame both held
me back and made the kiss
less bold and slow to come.
But while that sweetness sank
within my heart, mixed with
an unknown pois'nous brew,
such great delight had I,
that feigning that the pain brought by my bite
had not yet passed away,
I made her reapply
her magic more than once.
From then to now desire and suffering
have been increasing so, my breast could not
contain them both: I was compelled to burst.
And then there was another time when all
the nymphs and shepherds sat within a ring
and played our games as we were wont to do,
and each did whisper in his neighbor's ear,
and murmuring did tell his secret there.
"My Silvia," I said, "I burn for you
and sure will die if you don't grant me aid."
On hearing this, she lowered her lovely head
and on it spread a rare and sudden blush,
which gave away her anger and her shame:
she gave me no reply but silence then,
a silence wrought — and full — of threatening.
She left me then and has not wished to see
me nor to hear me more. And now three times

ha il nudo mietitor tronche le spighe,
ed altrettante il verno ha scossi i boschi
de le lor verdi chiome: ed ogni cosa
tentata ho per placarla, fuor che morte.
Mi resta sol che per placarla io mora:
e morrò volontier, pur ch'io sia certo
ch'ella o se ne compiaccia, o se ne doglia:
né so di tai due cose qual più brami.
Ben fora la pietà premio maggiore
a la mia fede, e maggior ricompensa
a la mia morte; ma bramar non deggio
cosa che turbi il bel lume sereno
a gli occhi cari, e affanni quel bel petto.

TIRSI

È possibil però che, s'ella un giorno
udisse tai parole, non t'amasse?

AMINTA

Non so, né 'l credo; ma fugge i miei detti
come l'aspe l'incanto.

TIRSI

Or ti confida,
ch'a me dà il cuor di far ch'ella t'ascolti.

AMINTA

O nulla impetrerai, o, se tu impetri
ch'io parli, io nulla impetrerò parlando.

TIRSI

Perché disperi sì?

the naked reaper's cut the cornstalks down,
and winter's freed the trees another three
of their green crown of leaves, and I've tried all
I know to placate her, except to die.
And now to placate her, I've got to die,
and willingly I'll die, if I were sure
that it would please her or that she would grieve,
nor know I which of these I would desire.
The greater prize to offer to my faith
and greater recompense for death would be
her pity, but I must not want a thing
that would disturb the soft light of her eyes,
so dear, and sore afflict that lovely breast.

TIRSI

Can it be possible that she would hear
such words someday and not be moved to love?

AMINTA

Who knows? I can't believe it. But she flees
my words as asps flee magic arts.[14]

TIRSI

Now be calm,
for I shall try to make her hear your words.

AMINTA

Imploring can gain nothing, or if you
obtain consent, my words will count for naught.

TIRSI

Why do you so despair?

AMINTA

Giusta cagione
ho del disperar, che il saggio Mopso
mi predisse la mia cruda ventura,
Mopso ch'intende il parlar degli augelli
e la virtù de l'erbe e de le fonti.

TIRSI

Di qual Mopso tu dici? di quel Mopso
ch'ha ne la lingua melate parole,
e ne le labra un amichevol ghigno,
e la fraude nel seno, ed il rasoio
tien sotto il manto? Or su, sta di bon core,
che i sciaurati pronostici infelici
ch'ei vende a' mal accorti con quel grave
suo supercilio non han mai effetto:
e per prova so io ciò che ti dico;
anzi da questo sol ch'ei t'ha predetto
mi giova di sperar felice fine
a l'amor tuo.

AMINTA

Se sai cosa per prova,
che conforti mia speme, non tacerla.

TIRSI

Dirolla volontieri. Allor che prima
mia sorte mi condusse in queste selve,
costui conobbi, e lo stimava io tale
qual tu lo stimi; in tanto un dì mi venne
e bisogno e talento d'irne dove
siede la gran cittade in ripa al fiume,
ed a costui ne feci motto; ed egli

AMINTA

I have just cause
for desperation: once wise Mopso spoke
and he foretold my cruel, cruel fate.
He understands the language of the birds,
the powers of herbs, and virtues of the springs.

TIRSI

What Mopso do you speak of?[15] Mopso, who
has honeyed words forever on his tongue
while on his lips he wears a friendly grin
and carries fraud within his breast and blades
beneath his coat? Come on, for heaven's sake,
for those unhappy, damnèd prophecies
he sells to rash, imprudent men with grave
and haughty airs, will never take effect.
I'm telling you I know that for a fact.
In fact, because he has predicted this,
it makes me hope your love will have an end
that's joyous and glad.

AMINTA

If you know things
to raise my halting hope, do not be quiet.

TIRSI

I'll tell you willingly. When first my fate
did draw me forth into these sylvan glades,
I knew him, and I thought of him as you
esteem him now. Meanwhile one day I had
the need and the desire to go down where
the city sits upon the river's bank,
and I told him my plan, and he replied,

così mi disse: "Andrai ne la gran terra,
ove gli astuti e scaltri cittadini
e i cortigian malvagi molte volte
prendonsi a gabbo, e fanno brutti scherni
di noi rustici incauti; però, figlio,
va su l'avviso, e non t'appressar troppo
ove sian drappi colorati e d'oro
e pennacchi e divise e foggie nove;
ma sopra tutto guarda che mal fato
o giovenil vaghezza non ti meni
al magazzino de le ciancie: ah, fuggi,
fuggi quel'incantato alloggiamento."
"Che luogo è questo?" io chiesi; ed ei soggiunse:
"Quivi abitan le maghe, che incantando
fan traveder e traudir ciascuno.
Ciò che diamante sembra ed oro fino,
è vetro e rame; e quelle arche d'argento,
che stimeresti piene di tesoro,
sporte son piene di vesciche bugge.
Quivi le mura son fatte con arte,
che parlano e rispondono a i parlanti:
né già rispondon la parola mozza,
com'Eco suole ne le nostre selve,
ma la replican tutta intiera intiera:
con giunta anco di quel ch'altri non disse.
I trespidi, le tavole e le panche,
le scranne, le lettiere, le cortine,
e gli arnesi di camera e di sala
han tutti lingua e voce: e gridan sempre.
Quivi le ciancie in forma di bambine
vanno trescando, e se un muto v'entrasse,
un muto ciancerebbe a suo dispetto.
Ma questo è 'l minor mal che ti potesse

"Now you are going to the teeming town
where sly and clever citizens abide
and wicked courtiers who often make
a jest, or laugh in cruel mockery
at careless rustics such as we. But, son,
be on your guard, and do not go too near
a place where colored cloth and cloth of gold
hang thick, and plumes and strange attire and modes;
but guard above all else that destiny
and young desire should never lead you to
the shop of nothing-is.[16] Ah! Flee the place,
fly far away from that enchanted spot."
"What place is this?" I asked; and he did add,
"Magicians there abide and do enchant
and veil the eyes and ears of those who come.
What seems to be of diamonds and fine gold
is glass and copper; and those silver arks,
which you would think are full of treasures rare,
are baskets full of empty bladder bags.
Down there the walls are made with magic art;
they speak and answer those who speak to them;
they don't respond with half a word or phrase,
as Echo often answers in our wood,
but they reply with words complete, complete,
and even phrases others did not say.
The stools, the tables, even every bench,
the high-backed chairs, the bedsteads and the drapes,
the objects of the bed- and living-rooms,
they all have tongues and speech and always shout.
There gossips go like dancing girls and weave
intrigues; and if a mute man entered there,
he'd chatter on although he'd rather not.
But this is still the least ill that you could

incontrar: tu potresti indi restarne
converso in selce, in fera, in acqua, o in foco:
acqua di pianto, e foco di sospiri."
Così diss'egli: ed io n'andai con questo
fallace antiveder ne la cittade;
e, come volse il Ciel benigno, a caso
passai per là dov'è 'l felice albergo.
Quindi uscian fuor voci canore e dolci
e di cigni e di ninfe e di sirene,
di sirene celesti; e n'uscian suoni
soavi e chiari; e tanto altro diletto,
ch'attonito godendo ed ammirando
mi fermai buona pezza. Era su l'uscio,
quasi per guardia de le cose belle,
uom d'aspetto magnanimo e robusto,
di cui, per quanto intesi, in dubbio stassi
s'egli sia miglior duce o cavaliero;
che, con fronte benigna insieme e grave,
con regal cortesia invitò dentro,
ei grande e 'n pregio, me negletto e basso.
Oh che sentii? che vidi allora? I' vidi
celesti dee, ninfe leggiadre e belle,
novi Lini ed Orfei; ed oltre ancora,
senza vel, senza nube, e quale e quanta
agl'immortali appar, vergine Aurora
sparger d'argento e d'or rugiade e raggi;
e fecondando illuminar d'intorno
vidi Febo, e le Muse; e fra le Muse
Elpin seder accolto; ed in quel punto
sentii me far di me stesso maggiore
pien di nova virtù, pieno di nova
deitade, e cantai guerre ed eroi,
sdegnando pastoral ruvido carme.

meet there: you could stay there forever changed
to flint, to beasts, to water, or to fire;
the water comes from tears, from sighs the fire."
That's what he said, and I went forth with this
fallacious vision of th' enchanted town;
and, just as heaven willed that it should be,
by chance I passed the place that he'd described.
From there came forth, melodious and sweet,
the mingled songs of sirens, swans, and nymphs,
celestial siren sounds, such sounds they were,
so soft and clear and full of fine delight,
that all astonished, wondering and enjoying,
I stopped for quite a time. Before the door,
as if a guard of things so fine and rare,
there was a man, magnanimous and strong,
and I could not decide, how hard I looked,
were he a cavalier or general,
for with a smile both grave and so benign,
he did invite me in with regal grace —
he so grand and fine, I, worthless, low.
What did I hear? What did I see? I saw
divinities; graceful, pretty nymphs;
new Orfeos and Linuses, and more —
Aurora, virgin Dawn, without a cloud
or veil, as she appears before the gods
to strew sun rays with gold and silver dew;
and fertile Phoebus and the Muses, then
I saw, illumining the scene; and there,
among the Muses, Elpin sat; and then
I felt myself become a greater man
infused with newfound strength, infused with a
new deity, and sang of wars and men,
disdaining rustic shepherds' songs and lays.

E se ben poi (come altrui piacque) feci
ritorno a queste selve, io pur ritenni
parte di quello spirto: né già suona
la mia sampogna umil come soleva:
ma di voce più altera e più sonora,
emula de le trombe, empie le selve.
Udimmi Mopso poscia; e con maligno
guardo mirando affascinommi: ond'io
roco divenni, e poi gran tempo tacqui:
quando i pastor credean ch'io fossi stato
visto dal lupo, e 'l lupo era costui.
Questo t'ho detto, acciò che sappi quanto
il parlar di costui di fede è degno:
e déi bene sperar, sol perché ei vuole
che nulla speri.

AMINTA

Piacemi d'udire
quanto mi narri. A te dunque rimetto
la cura di mia vita.

TIRSI

Io n'avrò cura.
Tu fra mezz'ora qui trovar ti lassa.

CORO

O bell'età de l'oro,
non già perché di latte
sen' corse il fiume e stillò mele il bosco;
non perché i frutti loro
dier da l'aratro intatte
le terre, e gli angui errâr senz'ira o tosco;
non perché nuvol fosco

And if I then returned, as others asked,
to these retreats, I've still retained a part
of that proud spirit here; nor have I played
my humble shepherd's pipes, as once I did,
but with more sonorous and proud a voice
I filled the forest with my trumpet tones.
Then later Mopso heard me and he fixed
me with his evil stare, and after I
was hoarse and silent for a long, long time.[17]
The shepherds thus believed that I had been
seen by the wolf, but it was really he.[18]
I've told you this so you will know how much
the speech he makes is worthy of your trust,
and just because he wants no one to hope,
you should have hope.

AMINTA

It pleases me to hear
all that you've told to me. I therefore trust
my life to you.

TIRSI

And I'll take care of you.
Come meet me here within a half an hour.

CHORUS

Oh, first fair age of gold,
not just because streams ran
with milk, and trees the honeyed dew distilled;
nor that the earth did mold
its fruit from unploughed land
and serpents roamed no ire nor venom filled;
no dark cloud ever chilled,

non spiegò allor suo velo,
ma in primavera eterna,
ch'ora s'accende e verna,
rise di luce e di sereno il cielo;
né portò peregrino
o guerra o merce a gli altrui lidi il pino;

ma sol perché quel vano
nome senza soggetto,
quell'idolo d'errori, idol d'inganno,
quel che dal volgo insano
onor poscia fu detto,
che di natura 'l feo tiranno,
non mischiava il suo affanno
fra le liete dolcezze
de l'amoroso gregge;
né fu sua dura legge
nota a quell'alme in libertate avvezze,
ma legge aurea e felice
che natura scolpì: S'ei piace, ei lice.

Allor tra fiori e linfe
traen dolci carole
gli Amoretti senz'archi e senza faci;
sedean pastori e ninfe
meschiando a le parole
vezzi e sussurri, ed a i susurri i baci
strettamente tenaci;
la verginella ignude
scopria sue fresche rose,
ch'or tien nel velo ascose,
e le poma del seno acerbe e crude;
e spesso in fonte o in lago
scherzar si vide con l'amata il vago.

nor close to earth did cling;
the skies that now inflame
or chill smiled light, serene
in an eternal spring;
and frigates never bore
to alien shores nor pilgrims, freight, nor war.

But just because that vain
abstraction, empty word,
that erring idol of propriety —
which was by folk, insane,
as *Honor* since referred —
which tyrannizes now society,
mixed not anxiety
within the happy joy
of loving's faithful band;
nor was its harsh command
known by those souls who liberty employed,
but nature's law of gold
and joy, *do what pleases you,* was told.

Then through the grassy glades
sang sweetly soft the song
of bowless, torchless cupids[19] — such was this:
sat shepherds there, and maids,
words mingling all along
with touches and murmurs, murmurs with a kiss
in closely clinging bliss;
the virgin maid, undressed,
disclosed her dewy rose,
which now we veil and close,
and showed the unpicked apples of her breast;
and oft in lake or stream
her lover frolicking with her was seen.

Tu prima, Onor, velasti
la fonte dei diletti,
negando l'onde a l'amorosa sete;
tu a' begli occhi insegnasti
di starne in sé ristretti,
e tener lor bellezze altrui secrete;
tu raccogliesti in rete
le chiome a l'aura sparte;
tu i dolci atti lascivi
festi ritrosi e schivi;
ai detti il fren ponesti, ai passi l'arte;
opra è tua sola, o Onore,
che furto sia quel che fu don d'Amore.

E son tuoi fatti egregi
le pene e i pianti nostri.
Ma tu, d'Amore e di Natura donno,
tu domator de' Regi,
che fai tra questi chiostri
che la grandezza tua capir non ponno?
Vattene, e turba il sonno
agl'illustri e potenti:
noi qui, negletta e bassa
turba, senza te lassa
viver ne l'uso de l'antiche genti.
Amiam, che non ha tregua
con gli anni umana vita, e si dilegua.

Amiam, che 'l Sol si muore e poi rinasce:
a noi sua breve luce
s'asconde, e 'l sonno eterna notte adduce.

You, Honor, first you hid
the fount of love's delight,
denying drafts to slake the lover's thirst;
to lovely eyes you bid
restraint or even flight
to keep their beauties' charms in secrets cursed;
in nets you gathered first
their hair spread on the breeze;
sweet, wanton acts, so dear
you made coy and shy appear;
you stopped plain words, filled steps with modesties;
this, Honor, was your deed
that stole the gifts that Love for us decreed.[20]

Your great accomplishments
are pains and tears for us.
But you, the Lord of Love and Natural Right,
who rules great kings' intents,
why are you acting thus
when once no cloister held your power and might?
Go shake the sleep at night
of all the great and bold;
and us, forgotten, low,
you let us live and go
the happy way that lived the men of old.
Let's love, for with the years
man's life can have no truce, and disappears.

Let's love, for day will die, yet is reborn;
for us, though, all its light
sinks down, and sleep leads to eternal night.

Aminta

Intermedio Primo

Proteo son io, che trasmutar sembianti
e forme soglio variar sì spesso;
e trovai l'arte onde notturna scena
cangia l'apetto; e quinci Amore istesso
trasforma in tante guise i vaghi amanti,
com'ogni carme ed ogni storia è piena.
Ne la notte serena,
ne l'amico silenzio e ne l'orrore,
sacro marin pastore
vi mostra questo coro e questa pompa;
né vien chi l'interrompa,
e turbi i nostri giuochi e i nostri canti.

Interlude One

I'm Proteus, and in many a way
I often change my form and how I look;
I've found the art whereby a nighttime scene
can be transformed: from me his power Love took
to change fair lovers many ways, as say
so many songs, and story plots oft mean.
And in the night, serene,
in friendly silence and in sacred awe,
divine sea shepherd, I
reveal this dancing chorus and this show.
Let none disturb us, no,
nor interrupt our games and tuneful lay.

Aminta

Atto Secondo

Scena Prima
Satiro solo

Satiro

Piccola è l'ape, e fa col picciol morso
pur gravi e pur moleste le ferite;
ma qual cosa è più picciola d'Amore,
se in ogni breve spazio entra, e s'asconde
in ogni breve spazio? or sotto a l'ombra
de le palpebre, or tra' minuti rivi
d'un biondo crine, or dentro le pozzette
che forma un dolce riso in bella guancia;
e pur fa tanto grandi e sì mortali
e così immedicabili le piaghe.
Ohimè, che tutte piaga e tutte sangue
son le viscere mie; e mille spiedi
ha ne gli occhi di Silvia il crudo Amore.
Crudel Amor, Silvia crudele ed empia
più che le selve! Oh come a te confassi
tal nome, e quanto vide chi te 'l pose!
Celan le selve angui, leoni ed orsi
dentro il lor verde: e tu dentro al bel petto
nascondi odio, disdegno ed impietate:
fere peggior ch'angui, leoni ed orsi:
che si placano quei, questi placarsi
non possono per prego né per dono.
Ohimè, quando ti porto i fior novelli,
tu li ricusi, ritrosetta: forse
perché fior via più belli hai nel bel volto.
Ohimè, quando io ti porgo i vaghi pomi,
tu li rifiuti, disdegnosa: forse

Act Two

Scene One
Satyr

Satyr

The bee is tiny, and with tiny bites
that hurt and that annoy stings its prey;
but what thing can be named that's tinier
than Love, if in so small a space he comes,
and in so small a space he hides? Now in
the eyelids' shade, now in the minute streams
of golden curls, now deep in dimples that
form such sweet smiles in lovely maiden cheeks;
and yet he makes a mortal wound so great
that medicine could never hope to cure.
O God! How hard he wounds and breaks my heart,
this cruel Love, who's placed a thousand shafts
within the eyes of Silvia for me.
Most cruel Love! And cruel Silvia,
worse than sylvan wilds! Oh, how your name
is fitting, just as he who gave it knew![21]
The woods hide serpents, lions, and even bears
within their green, and you within your breast
hide hate, disdain, and lack of pity — beasts
far worse than serpents, lions, or even bears:
for those may be appeased, but your disdain
cannot be soothed by praise or any gift.
Alas! When I bring tender flowers there,
you turn them down, disdainful girl, perhaps
because far fairer flowers deck your face.
Alas! When I bring pretty apples there,
you turn them down, O spiteful girl, perhaps

perché pomi più vaghi hai nel bel seno.
Lasso, quand'io t'offrisco il dolce mele,
tu lo disprezzi, dispettosa: forse
perché mel via più dolce hai ne le labra.
Ma, se mia povertà non può donarti
cosa ch'in te non sia più bella e dolce,
me medesmo ti dono. Or perché iniqua
scherni ed abborri il dono? non son io
da disprezzar, se ben me stesso vidi
nel liquido del mar, quando l'altr'ieri
taceano i venti ed ei giacea senz'onda.
Questa mia faccia di color sanguigno,
queste mie spalle larghe, e queste braccia
torose e nerborute, e questo petto
setoso, e queste mie velate coscie
son di virilità, di robustezza
indicio: e, se no 'l credi, fanne prova.
Che vuoi tu far di questi tenerelli
che di molle lanugine fiorite
hanno a pena le guancie? e che con arte
dispongono i capelli in ordinanza?
Femine nel sembiante e ne le forze
sono costoro. Or di' ch'alcun ti segua
per le selve e pei monti, e 'ncontra gli orsi
ed incontra i cinghiai per te combatta.
Non sono io brutto, no, né tu mi sprezzi
perché sì fatto io sia, ma solamente
perché povero sono; ahi, che le ville
seguon l'essempio de le gran cittadi;
e veramente il secol d'oro è questo,
poiché sol vince l'oro e regna l'oro.
O chiunque tu fosti, che insegnasti
primo a vender l'amor, sia maledetto

because far fairer apples are your breasts.
Alas! When honey sweet I offer you,
you scorn the gift, O spiteful girl, perhaps
because far sweeter honey's in your lips.
But if my lack can never offer you
a thing that you don't have more sweet and fair,
I offer you myself. Now why, unjust,
do you abhor and scorn my gift? I am
not one to scorn, although I saw myself
reflected in the liquid sea, when winds
were quiet the other day and made no waves.
This face of mine is ruddy-hued withal,
my shoulders great and large, my sturdy arms
robust and muscular, my chest is thick
with hair, and these, my hairy thighs, are all
an indication of virility
and strength: I'll prove it if you don't believe.
What would you have with tender little boys
like these whose cheeks are scarcely flowered with
the softest down? And who so artfully
arrange their hair according to the mode?
These men are feminine in semblance
and in strength. Now say, if one should follow you
through woods and hills, and there encounter bears
and meet wild boars, would he fight them for you?
I am not ugly, no; and you do not
despise me for my shape, but just because
I'm poor. Alas, for even villages
do take the model of the cities' mode!
And this is rightly called the golden age,
since gold alone can conquer and can reign.
O you, who were the first to teach that love
be sold, whoe'er you were, be damned your bones,

il tuo cener sepolto e l'ossa fredde,
e non si trovi mai pastore o ninfa
che lor dica passando: "Abbiate pace";
ma le bagni la pioggia e mova il vento,
e con pié immondo la greggia il calpesti
e 'l peregrin. Tu prima svergognasti
la nobiltà d'amor; tu le sue liete
dolcezze inamaristi. Amor venale,
amor servo de l'oro è il maggior mostro
ed il più abominabile e il più sozzo
che produca la terra o 'l mar fra l'onde.
Ma perché in van mi lagno? Usa ciascuno
quell'armi che gli ha date la natura
per sua salute: il cervo adopra il corso,
il leone gli artigli, ed il bavoso
cinghiale il dente; e son potenza ed armi
de la donna bellezza e leggiadria;
io, perché non per mia salute adopro
la violenza, se mi fé Natura
atto a far violenza ed a rapire?
Sforzerò, rapirò quel che costei
mi niega, ingrata, in merto de l'amore:
che, per quanto un caprar testé mi ha detto,
ch'osservato ha suo stile, ella ha per uso
d'andar sovente a rinfrescarsi a un fonte:
e mostrato m'ha il loco. Ivi io disegno
tra i cespugli appiattarmi e tra gli arbusti,
ed aspettar fin che vi venga; e, come
veggia l'occasion, correrle adosso.
Qual contrasto col corso e con le braccia
potrà fare una tenera fanciulla
contra me sì veloce e sì possente?
Pianga e sospiri pure, usi ogni sforzo

be damned your frigid ashes in the earth,
and would there were no nymphs and shepherds who
in passing say to you, "Oh, may you rest in peace";
oh, rather rain should bathe and wind should howl
about you, and the dirty feet of flocks
and pilgrims trample you. You first disgraced
love's noble name and turned to bitterness
its sweetest joys. Now venal Love, now Love
the slave of gold's become the monstrous beast,
the most abominable and foulest thing
that earth or wave-tossed sea has yet brought forth.
But why lament in vain? For safety each
should use those arms that nature gave to him:
the deer employs running, and the lion
will use his claws; the wild boar, slobbering,
will use his teeth; and grace and beauty are
the power and the arms a woman bears.
And I, why don't I use for my own good
raw violence, if it's true that nature made
me in a mold for violence and rapine?
I'll force, I'll rape, I'll take what she denies
ungratefully, as my reward of love.
Now, recently a goatherd told me that
he had observed her ways: she often goes
to rest and cool herself nearby a spring —
and he has shown the place. It's there I plan
to hide myself amid the shrubs and trees,
and there I'll wait for her; and when the time
is right, I'll spring and take her by surprise.
What opposition with her swiftness and
her arm could such a tender maiden make
against a man so swift and strong as I?
Then let her cry and sigh, use every force

di pietà, di bellezza: che, s'io posso
questa mano ravvoglierle nel crine,
indi non partirà, ch'io pria non tinga
l'armi mie per vendetta nel suo sangue.

SCENA SECONDA
DAFNE, TIRSI

DAFNE

Tirsi, com'io t'ho detto, io m'era accorta
ch'Aminta amava Silvia, e Dio sa quanti
buoni officii n'ho fatti, e son per farli
tanto più volontier quant'or vi aggiungi
le tue preghiere; ma torrei più tosto
a domar un giuvenco, un orso, un tigre,
che a domar una semplice fanciulla:
fanciulla tanto sciocca quanto bella,
che non s'avveggia ancor come sian calde
l'armi di sua bellezza, e come acute:
ma ridendo e piangendo uccida altrui,
e l'uccida e non sappia di ferire.

TIRSI

Ma quale è così semplice fanciulla
che, uscita da le fascie, non apprenda
l'arte del parer bella e del piacere,
de l'uccider piacendo, e del sapere
qual arme fera, e qual dia morte, e quale
sani e ritorni in vita?

DAFNE

Chi è 'l mastro
di cotant'arte?

of pity or of beauty, for if I
can wrap her hair around this hand of mine,
then she'll not leave until my arms are dyed
and reddened by her blood for vengeance sake.

Scene Two
Dafne and Tirsi

Dafne

Tirsi, as I've said I was aware
Aminta loved her well; and God knows how
I've talked to her for him, and I'll still speak
more willingly now that you'll add your prayers
to those I make; but I would rather try
to tame a steer, a tiger, or a bear,
than try to tame a simple, prideful girl,
a girl who's foolish as she's beautiful,
who still can't realize the weapons that
her beauty bears are powerful and sharp,
but laughing, weeping slays another soul,
and slays him though she knows not how to wound.[22]

Tirsi

But where's the girl so simple that, come forth
from swaddling clothes, can't apprehend the art
of being beautiful, of pleasure's drift,
of slaying that is sweet, and knowing which
arms wound and which give death and which restore
the dead to life!

Dafne

Who is the master of
such arts as these?

Tirsi

Tu fingi, e mi tenti:
quel che insegna agli augelli il canto e 'l volo,
a' pesci il nuoto ed a' montoni il cozzo,
al toro usar il corno, ed al pavone
spiegar la pompa de l'occhiute piume.

Dafne

Come ha nome 'l gran mastro?

Tirsi

Dafne ha nome.

Dafne

Lingua bugiarda!

Tirsi

E perché? tu non sei
atta a tener mille fanciulle a scola?
Benché, per dir il ver, non han bisogno
di maestro: maestra è la natura,
ma la madre e la balia anco v'han parte.

Dafne

In somma, tu sei goffo insieme e tristo.
Ora, per dirti il ver, non mi risolvo
se Silvia è semplicetta come pare
a le parole, agli atti. Ier vidi un segno
che me ne mette in dubbio. Io la trovai
là presso la cittade in quei gran prati
ove fra stagni giace un'isoletta,
sovra essa un lago limpido e tranquillo,
tutta pendente, in atto che parea

TIRSI

You test me and pretend.
It's she who teaches birds to sing and fly,
the fishes how to swim and rams to butt,
the bull to use its horns and peacocks how
to spread the splendor of their star-eyed plumes.

DAFNE

And what's this master's name?

TIRSI

She's Dafne called.

DAFNE

O lying tongue.

TIRSI

And why? Are you not fit
to hold a school for e'en a thousand girls?
Although, to tell the truth, they have no need
of teachers: nature teaches them these things,
but mothers and their nurse may take a part.

DAFNE

You wicked man, you're bashful as you're mean.
To tell the truth, I've not decided yet
if Silvia is simple as she seems
in words and deeds. For yesterday I saw
a sign that gave me doubts. I saw her there,
nearby the city walls in those great fields
where midst the pools there lies a little isle;
she pendant stood above the limpid lake's
smooth calm and seemed to take delight in her

vagheggiar se medesma, e 'nsieme insieme
chieder consiglio a l'acque in qual maniera
dispor dovesse in su la fronte i crini,
e sovra i crini il velo, e sovra 'l velo
i fior che tenea in grembo; e spesso spesso
ora prendeva un ligustro, or una rosa,
e l'accostava al bel candido collo,
a le guancie vermiglie, e de' colori
fea paragone: e poi, sì come lieta
de la vittoria, lampeggiava un riso
che parea che dicesse: "Io pur vi vinco,
né porto voi per ornamento mio,
ma porto voi sol per vergogna vostra,
perché si veggia quanto mi cedete."
Ma, mentre ella s'ornava e vagheggiava,
rivolse gli occhi a caso, e si fu accorta
ch'io di lei m'era accorta, e vergognando
rizzossi tosto, e i fior lasciò cadere.
In tanto io più ridea del suo rossore,
ella più s'arrossia del riso mio.
Ma, perché accolta una parte de' crini
e l'altra aveva sparsa, una o due volte
con gli occhi al fonte consiglier ricorse,
e si mirò quasi di furto, pure
temendo ch'io nel suo guatar guatassi;
ed incolta si vide, e si compiacque
perché bella si vide ancor che incolta.
Io me n'avvidi, e tacqui.

TIRSI

Tu mi narri
quel ch'io credeva a punto. Or non m'apposi?

reflection — at the self same time she seemed
to ask the water counsel in what way
she should arrange her hair about her face
and on her hair the veil, and on the veil
the flowers she held; and frequent, frequently
she took a sprig of green, and now a rose
and linked them 'round her lovely, candid neck,
upon vermilion cheeks, a paragon
of their soft tint; and then delighted as
in victory, a smile lit up her face
as if to say, "It's I who conquer you;
nor do I wear you for my ornament,
but I do wear you only for your shame,
because you see how much you yield to me."
While she, adorning, gazed adoringly,
she raised her eyes by chance and was aware
that I had seen her there, and all ashamed,
she quickly stood and let the flowers fall.
And all the while, the more her blush amused,
the more she reddened at my laughing smile.
A part of her bright hair was gathered tight,
the other had dispersed, and it was thus
that once or twice her eyes sought out the lake —
her image there — though furtively she glanced,
afraid, perhaps, that at her gaze gazed I:
she saw herself in disarray and smiled,
for she was beautiful though disarrayed.
I noticed and was quiet.

TIRSI

You're telling me
just what I thought. Now didn't I guess right?

DAFNE

Ben t'apponesti; ma pur odo dire
che non erano pria le pastorelle
né le ninfe sì accorte; né io tale
fui in mia fanciullezza. Il mondo invecchia,
ed invecchiando intristisce.

TIRSI

Forse allora
non usavan sì spesso i cittadini
ne le selve e nei campi, né sì spesso
le nostre forosette aveano in uso
d'andare a la cittade. Or son mischiate
schiatte e costumi. Ma lasciam da parte
questi discorsi: or non farai ch'un giorno
Silvia contenta sia che le ragioni
Aminta, o solo, o almeno in tua presenza?

DAFNE

Non so. Silvia è ritrosa fuor di modo.

TIRSI

E costui rispettoso è fuor di modo.

DAFNE

È spacciato un amante rispettoso:
consiglial pur che faccia altro mestiero,
poich'egli è tal. Chi imparar vuol d'amare,
disimpari il rispetto: osi, domandi,
solleciti, importuni, al fine involi;
e se questo non basta, anco rapisca.
Or non sai tu com'è fatta la donna?
Fugge, e fuggendo vuol che altri la giunga;

Act Two, Scene Two

DAFNE

You guessed quite well. But I have heard it said
that neither shepherd girls nor nymphs were once
as shrewd as that, nor was I such a one
in my girlhood. This world of ours grows old,
and growing old, grows sad.

TIRSI

In distant days
perhaps the city folk did not come here
among the wood and fields so much, nor were
our country girls so often used to go
within the city walls. Now stocks are mixed,
and customs too. But let us leave aside
these thoughts awhile. Can you arrange one day
that Silvia will gladly hear the words
Aminta speaks, alone, or with you there?

DAFNE

I do not know. For Silvia's too shy.

TIRSI

And his respectfulness is far too great.

DAFNE

A lover too respectful is undone.
I counsel him to work at something else,
since he is such a one. Who wants to learn
to love, forget respect: you dare, demand,
solicit, importune, and finally steal;
and if that's not enough, then ravish her.
Now don't you know how woman is designed?
She flees and fleeing wants to soon be caught;

niega, e negando vuol ch'altri si toglia;
pugna, e pugnando vuol ch'altri la vinca.
Ve', Tirsi, io parlo teco in confidenza:
non ridir ch'io ciò dica. E sovra tutto
non porlo in rime. Tu sai s'io saprei
renderti poi per versi altro che versi.

TIRSI

Non hai cagion di sospettar ch'io dica
cosa giamai che sia contra tuo grado.
Ma ti prego, o mia Dafne, per la dolce
memoria di tua fresca giovanezza,
che tu m'aiti ad aitar Aminta
miserel, che si muore.

DAFNE

Oh che gentile
scongiuro ha ritrovato questo sciocco
di rammentarmi la mia giovanezza,
il ben passato e la presente noia!
Ma che vuoi tu ch'io faccia?

TIRSI

A te non manca
né saper né consiglio. Basta sol che
ti disponga a voler.

DAFNE

Or su, dirotti:
debbiamo in breve andare Silvia ed io
al fonte che s'appella di Diana,
là dove a le dolci acque fa dolce ombra
quel platano ch'invita al fresco seggio

says no and saying wants to give herself;
she fights and fighting wants the man to win.
See, Tirsi, this I say in confidence.
Don't laugh at what I say; especially
don't put it down in rhyme. You know that I'd
know how to pay you back with verse for verse.

TIRSI

You have no cause to think that I
would say a thing that is against your wish;
but, O my Dafne, please, for that sweet thought,
the memory of the freshness of your youth,
help me, and help Aminta, that poor fool,
for he is dying.

DAFNE

Oh, how gentle is
the supplication this young fool has found
by just reminding me of my sweet youth,
the joyful past and present loneliness!
What would you have me do?

TIRSI

You do not lack
the knowledge or good counsel: you'll do well
to do just what you think.

DAFNE

Now up, I say:
for soon we'll go to Silvia and I
will go up to Diana's spring, there where
the plane tree casts its shadows sweet above
the silky wave and there invites to that

le ninfe cacciatrici. Ivi so certo
che tufferà le belle membra ignude.

TIRSI

Ma che però?

DAFNE

Ma che però? Da poco
intenditor! s'hai senno, tanto basti.

TIRSI

Intendo; ma non so s'egli avrà tanto
d'ardir.

DAFNE

S'ei non l'avrà, stiasi, ed aspetti
ch'altri lui cerchi.

TIRSI

Egli è ben tal che 'l merta.

DAFNE

Ma non vogliamo noi parlar alquanto
di te medesmo? Or su, Tirsi, non vuoi
tu inamorarti? sei giovane ancora,
né passi di quattr'anni il quinto lustro,
se ben sovviemmi quando eri fanciullo:
vuoi viver neghittoso e senza gioia?
che sol amando uom sa che sia diletto.

TIRSI

I diletti di Venere non lascia
l'uom che schiva l'amor, ma coglie e gusta
le dolcezze d'amor senza l'amaro.

fresh spot the huntress nymphs. I'm sure that there
she'll plunge her lovely body, nude, within.

TIRSI

But what comes then?

DAFNE

What then? Just now you were
an expert. If you have some sense, you'll know.

TIRSI

I understand; but I don't know if he
is brave enough.

DAFNE

If not, then let him stand
and wait until he's fetched.

TIRSI

He merits that.

DAFNE

But don't we want to speak of you a bit
yourself? So, Tirsi, tell me why you don't
desire to fall in love? For you're still young,
you haven't yet passed twenty-nine, I think,
if I remember when you were a boy.[23]
You want to live indifferent, without joy?
By loving only can man know delight.

TIRSI

The man who gives up love does not give up
all Venus' joys; he gathers up and tastes
love's sweet without the bitterness.

DAFNE

Insipido è quel dolce che condito
non è di qualche amaro, e tosto sazia.

TIRSI

È meglio saziarsi, ch'esser sempre
famelico nel cibo e dopo 'l cibo.

DAFNE

Ma non, se l'cibo si possede e piace,
e gustato a gustar sempre n'invoglia.

TIRSI

Ma chi possede sì quel che gli piace
che l'abbia sempre presso a la sua fame?

DAFNE

Ma chi ritrova il ben, s'egli no 'l cerca?

TIRSI

Periglioso è cercar quel che trovato
trastulla sì, ma più tormenta assai
non ritrovato. Allor vedrassi amante
Tirsi mai più, ch'Amor nel seggio suo
non avrà più né pianti né sospiri.
A bastanza ho già pianto e sospirato.
Faccia altri la sua parte.

DAFNE

Ma non hai
già goduto a bastanza.

Act Two, Scene Two

DAFNE

Insipid is that sweet that is not spiced
with bitter taste, and soon it's satisfied.

TIRSI

It's better to be satisfied than feel
an emptiness when eating — and when done.

DAFNE

But not if one has food that pleases so
that tasted once, it tempts to taste again.

TIRSI

But who possesses food that tastes so good
that he would always hunger after it?

DAFNE

But who will find the good if he won't search?

TIRSI

It's dangerous to search for that which, found,
amuses so, but torments more by far
if it's not found. Thus you will never see
Tirsi a lover more, for in his place
Love will put no tears or sighs again.
I've wept enough already, sighed enough;
let others have their share.

DAFNE

But you have not
enjoyed it enough.

TIRSI

Né desio
goder, se così caro egli si compra.

DAFNE

Sarà forza l'amar, se non fia voglia.

TIRSI

Ma non si può sforzar chi sta lontano.

DAFNE

Ma chi lung'è d'Amor?

TIRSI

Chi teme e fugge.

DAFNE

E che giova fuggir da lui, ch'ha l'ali?

TIRSI

Amor nascente ha corte l'ali: a pena
può su tenerle, e non le spiega a volo.

DAFNE

Pur non s'accorge l'uom quand'egli nasce:
e, quando uom se n'accorge, è grande, e vola.

TIRSI

Non, s'altra volta nascer non l'ha visto.

DAFNE

Vedrem, Tirsi, s'avrai la fuga e gli occhi
come tu dici. Io ti protesto, poi
che fai del corridore e del cerviero,

TIRSI

Nor do I want
to so enjoy, if it is bought so dear.

DAFNE

Love's power is great, though you might seek escape.

TIRSI

But one who's far away cannot be forced.

DAFNE

But who is far from Love?

TIRSI

Who fears and flees.

DAFNE

But who can flee from one who's given wings?

TIRSI

The wings of youthful Love are short; they can
be scarcely held aloft and spread to fly.

DAFNE

A man is not aware when love is born;
and when man is aware, it's grown and flies.

TIRSI

Not so, if he's not seen it born before.

DAFNE

We'll see if you will have good eyes and flee
as, Tirsi, you declare. I'm warning you,
since you would be a racer or a lynx,

che, quando ti vedrò chieder aita,
non moverei, per aiutarti, un passo,
un dito, un detto, una palpebra sola.

TIRSI

Crudel, daratti il cor vedermi morto?
Se vuoi pur ch'ami, ama tu me: facciamo
l'amor d'accordo.

DAFNE

Tu mi scherni, e forse
non merti amante così fatta: ahi quanti
n'inganna il viso colorito e liscio!

TIRSI

Non burlo io, no; ma tu con tal protesto
non accetti il mio amor, pur come è l'uso
di tutte quante; ma, se non mi vuoi,
viverò senza amor.

DAFNE

Contento vivi
più che mai fossi, o Tirsi, in ozio vivi,
e ne l'ozio l'amor sempre germoglia.

TIRSI

O Dafne, a me quest'ozii ha fatto Dio:
colui che Dio qui può stimarsi; a cui
si pascon gli ampi armenti e l'ampie greggie
da l'uno a l'altro mare, e per li lieti
colti di fecondissime campagne,
e per gli alpestri dossi d'Appennino.
Egli mi disse, allor che suo mi fece:
"Tirsi, altri scacci i lupi e i ladri, e guardi

that when I see you call for aid, I shall
not move a step to help, not speak a word,
not move a finger, and not blink an eye.

TIRSI

O cruel nymph, would you enjoy my death?
If you want me to love, then love me now;
let's love together now.

DAFNE

You scorn me, and
you don't deserve a love like mine. Ah, how
you men are fooled by smooth rose cheeks!

TIRSI

I do not jest; but you, with such pretext
do not accept my love, as women all
are wont. But if you don't desire my love,
I'll live without.

DAFNE

You'll live content more than
you did before; you'll live in indolence,
and love from leisure grows as sprouts a seed.

TIRSI

O Dafne, indolence was made for me
by one who here is thought a god, for whom
the ample herds and flocks do feed and graze
from one sea to the other, and throughout
the cultivated country's fecund fields,
and on the mountain crest of Apennines.[24]
He said to me (and after made me his):
"Some men do drive the wolves and thieves away

i miei murati ovili; altri comparta
le pene e i premii a' miei ministri; ed altri
pasca e curi le greggi; altri conservi
le lane e 'l latte, ed altri le dispensi:
tu canta, or che se' 'n ozio." Ond'è ben giusto
che non gli scherzi di terreno amore,
ma canti gli avi del mio vivo e vero
non so s'io lui mi chiami Apollo o Giove,
che ne l'opre e nel volto ambi somiglia:
gli avi più degni di Saturno o Celo;
agreste Musa a regal merto: e pure,
chiara o roca che suoni, ei non la sprezza.
Non canto lui, però che lui non posso
degnamente onorar se non tacendo
e riverendo: ma non fian giamai
gli altari suoi senza i miei fiori, e senza
soave fumo d'odorati incensi:
ed allor questa semplice e devota
religion mi si torrà dal core,
che d'aria pasceransi in aria i cervi,
e che, mutando i fiumi e letto e corso,
il Perso bea la Sona, il Gallo il Tigre.

DAFNE

Oh, tu vai alto: or su, discendi un poco
al proposito nostro.

TIRSI

Il punto è questo:
che tu in andando al fonte con colei,
cerchi d'intenerirla: ed io fra tanto
procurerò ch'Aminta là ne venga.
Né la mia forse men difficil cura
sarà di questa tua. Or vanne.

and guard my sheepfolds, Tirsi; others give
the pains and prizes to my ministers;
and others feed and mind the herds; the wool
and milk are kept by some; some give it out:
you sing, for you have leisure." Thus it's right
that you don't joke about terrestrial love,
but sing the fathers of my living god,
should he be called Apollo or great Jove,
for he resembles both in work and face,
the noblest ones of Saturn or of Sky.
O rustic Muse of regal gifts! Yet,
should you sing clear or hoarse, he'll not disdain.
I do not sing him, though, for I cannot
pay worthy honor but by silently
revering; but an altar's never raised
to him without my flowers and without
the pleasant smoke of incense smelling sweet.
And then this worship, simple and devout,
quite steals my heart away from me, and deer
fly feeding through the air, on air; the course
of rivers change their beds and flow; the Franks
drink from the Tigris, Persians from the Soane.[25]

DAFNE

Oh, ho! You're flying high! Come on, descend
a bit to our resolve.

TIRSI

The point is this:
that you should go up to the spring with her
and try to soften her, and meanwhile I
shall go and tell Aminta to go there:
perhaps my duty is more difficult
than yours will be. Now go.

DAFNE

Io vado,
ma il proposito nostro altro intendeva.

TIRSI

Se ben ravviso di lontan la faccia,
Aminta è quel che di là spunta. È desso.

SCENA TERZA
AMINTA, TIRSI

AMINTA

Vorrò veder ciò che Tirsi avrà fatto:
e, s'avrà fatto nulla,
prima ch'io vada in nulla
uccider vo' me stesso innanzi agli occhi
de la crudel fanciulla.
A lei, cui tanto piace
la piaga del mio core,
colpo de' suoi begli occhi,
altrettanto piacer devrà per certo
la piaga del mio petto,
colpo de la mia mano.

TIRSI

Nove, Aminta, t'annuncio di conforto:
lascia omai questo tanto lamentarti.

AMINTA

Oihmè, che di'? che porte?
O la vita o la morte?

DAFNE

I'm going now,
but our agreement was for other things.

TIRSI

If I can see his face from far away,
that is Aminta coming. Yes, it's he.

SCENE THREE
AMINTA AND TIRSI

AMINTA

I want to see what Tirsi's done for me;
and if it's nil he's done,
before to nil I go,
I want to kill myself before her eyes,
the cruel, cruel maid.
For she, who so dislikes
the wound made in my heart —
the blow of her fine eyes —
will surely like by just as great degree
the wound made in my breast —
the blow of my own hand.

TIRSI

Aminta, I have news to comfort you.
You do lament too much — leave it behind.

AMINTA

Alas! Is it the breath —
your speech — of life or death?

Tirsi

Porto salute e vita, s'ardirai
di farti loro incontra: ma fa d'uopo
d'esser un uom, Aminta, un uom ardito.

Aminta

Qual ardir mi bisogna, e 'ncontra a cui?

Tirsi

Se la tua donna fosse in mezz'un bosco
che, cinto intorno d'altissime rupi,
desse albergo a le tigri ed a' leoni,
v'andresti tu?

Aminta

V'andrei sicuro e baldo
più che di festa villanella al ballo.

Tirsi

E s'ella fosse tra ladroni ed armi,
v'andresti tu?

Aminta

V'andrei più lieto e pronto
che l'assetato cervo a la fontana.

Tirsi

Bisogna a maggior prova ardir più grande.

Aminta

Andrò per mezzo i rapidi torrenti
quando la neve si discioglie e gonfi
li manda al mare; andrò per mezzo 'l foco

TIRSI

I bring both health and life, if you will dare
to set yourself for them; but you must be
a man, Aminta, a courageous man.

AMINTA

What courage do I need, against what foe?

TIRSI

If she you love were deep within a wood,
and girded all around by towering rocks,
a refuge made for tigers and for lions,
would you go there?

AMINTA

More boldly I would go
than country maiden to the village dance.

TIRSI

And if she were surrounded by armed thieves,
would you go there?

AMINTA

I'd go more swift and glad
than to the fountain goes the thirsty deer.

TIRSI

This trial demands a courage greater still.

AMINTA

I'll go amid the rapid, flowing streams
when melting snows make torrents swell and send
them to the sea; I'll go amid the fire

e ne l'Inferno, quando ella vi sia,
s'esser può Inferno ov'è cosa sì bella.
Orsù, scuoprimi il tutto.

TIRSI

Odi.

AMINTA

Di' tosto.

TIRSI

Silvia t'attende a una fonte, ignuda e sola.
Ardirai tu d'andarvi?

AMINTA

Oh, che mi dici?
Silvia m'attende inguda e sola?

TIRSI

Sola,
se non quanto v'è Dafne, ch'è per noi.

AMINTA

Ignuda ella m'aspetta?

TIRSI

Ignuda: ma...

AMINTA

Ohimè, che ma*? Tu taci; tu m'uccidi.*

TIRSI

Ma non sa già che tu v'abbi d'andare.

and even into hell, if she be there,
if hell could be where one so lovely is.
Now tell it all to me.

TIRSI

Now hear.

AMINTA

Speak up.

TIRSI

She's waiting by a spring, alone and nude.
Dare you go there?

AMINTA

Oh, what is that you say?
Alone and nude, she waits for me?

TIRSI

Alone,
except for Dafne; but she's on our side.

AMINTA

She's nude, and waiting for me there?

TIRSI

Nude, yet...

AMINTA

Alas! Your "yets"! You're quiet; you're killing me.

TIRSI

She doesn't know that you are going there.

AMINTA

Dura conclusion, che tutte attosca
le dolcezze passate. Or, con qual arte,
crudel, tu mi tormenti?
Poco dunque ti pare
che infelice io sia,
che a crescer vieni la miseria mia?

TIRSI

S'a mio senno farai, sarai felice.

AMINTA

E che consigli?

TIRSI

Che tu prenda quello
che la fortuna amica t'appresenta.

AMINTA

Tolga Dio che mai faccia
cosa che le dispiaccia;
cosa io non feci mai che le spiacesse,
fuor che l'amarla: e questo a me fu forza,
forza di sua bellezza, e non mia colpa.
Non sarà dunque ver, ch'in quanto io posso
non cerchi compiacerla.

TIRSI

Ormai rispondi:
se fosse in tuo poter di non amarla,
lasciaresti d'amarla, per piacerle?

AMINTA

A grievous end that turns to bitterness
the sweet beginning. With what arts do you,
O cruel one, torment?
Then did it seem to you
when I was miserable
that you should come to make my mis'ry grow?

TIRSI

You would be happy, if you'd do my will.

AMINTA

And you would counsel me?

TIRSI

That you should take
what friendly fortune now presents to you.

AMINTA

God let me never do
a thing she'd disapprove.
I've never done a thing to anger her
except to love her. This was forced on me
by her own beauty and was not my fault.
It's true then that so far as I can do,
I've tried to please her.

TIRSI

Now then, answer me:
if it were in your power not to love,
would you stop loving her to please her whim?

AMINTA

Né questo mi consente Amor ch'io dica,
né ch'imagini pur d'aver già mai
a lasciar il suo amor, bench'io potessi.

TIRSI

Dunque tu l'ameresti al suo dispetto,
quando potessi far di non amarla.

AMINTA

Al suo dispetto no, ma l'amerei.

TIRSI

Dunque fuor di sua voglia.

AMINTA

Sì per certo.

TIRSI

Perché dunque non osi oltra sua voglia
prenderne quel che, se ben grava in prima,
al fin, al fin le sarà caro e dolce
che l'abbi preso?

AMINTA

Ahi, Tirsi, Amor risponda
per me; che quanto a mezz' il cor mi parla,
non so ridir. Tu troppo scaltro sei
già per lungo uso a ragionar d'amore:
a me lega la lingua
quel che mi lega il core.

TIRSI

Dunque andar non vogliamo?

Aminta

No. Love would never let me say such things
or even dream of ceasing loving her,
though I might wish that it could be that way.

Tirsi

Then you would love despite her own desire,
when you could act so not to love at all?

Aminta

Despite her, no; but I would love her still.

Tirsi

Then her will matters not?

Aminta

Oh yes, it does.

Tirsi

Then why don't you deny what her will wants,
and take that which, though hard for her at first,
will in the end be sweet and dear to her
when you have taken it?

Aminta

Ah, Tirsi, let
Love speak, for all he says within my heart,
I know not how to say. You are too sly
for having talked of love so long a time;
my tongue is tied by that
same thing that ties my heart.

Tirsi

Then don't you want to go?

AMINTA

Andare io voglio,
ma non dove tu stimi.

TIRSI

E dove?

AMINTA

A morte,
s'altro in mio pro' non hai fatto che quanto
ora mi narri.

TIRSI

E poco parti questo?
Credi tu dunque, sciocco, che mai Dafne
consigliasse l'andar, se non vedesse
in parte il cor di Silvia? E forse ch'ella
il sa, né però vuol ch'altri risappia
ch'ella ciò sappia. Or, se 'l consenso espresso
cerchi di lei, non vedi che tu cerchi
quel che più le dispiace? Or dove è dunque
questo tuo desiderio di piacerle?
E s'ella vuol che 'l tuo diletto sia
tuo furto o tua rapina, e non suo dono
né sua mercede, a te, folle, che importa
più l'un modo che l'altro?

AMINTA

E chi m'accerta
che il suo desir sia tale?

TIRSI

Oh mentecatto!
Ecco, tu chiedi pur quella certezza

AMINTA

I want to go,
but not there where you think.

TIRSI

So where?

AMINTA

To death,
if in my favor you've done nothing else
than what you say.

TIRSI

Then you would leave it so?
You fool, can you believe that Dafne would
suggest your going, if she did not see
a bit in Silvia's heart? It may be that
she knows it, yet would not have others know
just what she knows. Now if you seek express
consent from her, you're searching — can't you see —
for what displeases her? Now then, where is
this great desire of yours to please her will?
And if she wants that your delight should be
your theft or taking her by force, and not
her gift or offering to you, who cares
what way you do the deed?

AMINTA

And who assures
me her desire is such?

TIRSI

O half-wit fool!
Look here, you're still in search of certainty

ch'a lei dispiace, e dispiacer le deve
dirittamente, e tu cercar non déi.
Ma chi t'accerta ancor che non sia tale?
Or s'ella fosse tale, e non v'andassi?
Eguale è il dubbio, e 'l rischio. Ahi, pur è meglio
come ardito morir, che come vile.
Tu taci: tu sei vinto. Ora confessa
questa perdita tua, che fia cagione
di vittoria maggiore. Andianne.

AMINTA

Aspetta.

TIRSI

Che Aspetta? *non sai ben che 'l tempo fugge?*

AMINTA

Deh, pensiam pria se ciò dée farsi, e come.

TIRSI

Per strada penserem ciò che vi resta:
ma nulla fa chi troppe cose pensa.

CORO

Amore, in quale scola,
da qual mastro s'apprende
la tua sì lunga e dubbia arte d'amare?
Chi n'insegna a spiegare
ciò che la mente intende,
mentre con l'ali tue sovra il ciel vola?
Non già la dotta Atene,
né 'l Liceo ne 'l dimostra;
non Febo in Elicona,
che sì d'Amor ragiona

and that displeases her, and rightly so;
so certainties like that you shouldn't seek.
But who assures you that's the way she is?
If she were so, would you go there or not?
The risk and doubt are equal. Ah, it's best
to die courageous, than a coward die.
You're quiet; yes, you are conquered. Now confess
your loss that shall become the reason soon
of greater victory. Let's go now.

AMINTA

Wait.

TIRSI

Why wait? Aren't you aware that time flies on?

AMINTA

First think, should it be done, and if so, how?

TIRSI

We'll think along the road what's left to do,
but he who thinks too much gets nothing done.

CHORUS

O Love, where is the school,
from what professor did
we learn the lasting, dubious arts of love?
While in the sky above
our minds would fly, who bid
us come and learn about the realm you rule?
Not wise Athena, nor
her School could demonstrate;
not Phoebus on Mt. Helicon[26]
could speak of love, and reason on

come colui ch'impara:
freddo ne parla, e poco;
non ha voce di foco
come a te si conviene;
non alza i suoi pensieri
a par de' tuoi misteri.
Amor, degno maestro
sol tu sei di te stesso,
e sol tu sei da te medesmo espresso;
tu di lègger insegni
ai più rustici ingegni
quelle mirabil cose
che con lettre amorose
scrivi di propria man ne gli occhi altrui;
tu in bei facondi detti
sciogli la lingua de' fedeli tuoi;
e spesso (oh strana e nova
eloquenza d'Amore!)
spesso in un dir confuso
e 'n parole interrotte
meglio si esprime il core
e più par che si mova,
che non si fa con voci adorne e dotte;
e 'l silenzio ancor suole
aver prieghi e parole.

Amor, leggan pur gli altri
le socratiche carte,
ch'io in due begli occhi apprenderò quest'arte;
e perderan le rime
de le penne più saggie
appo le mie selvaggie,
che rozza mano in rozza scorza imprime.

of what you inculcate:
few words he spoke, did not inspire —
he lacked a voice filled with fire,
as you make sing and soar.
He could not raise his inmost thought
to match the mystery that you taught.
O worthy master, Love,
lord of yourself alone,
for you alone can teach us of your own.
You teach the rustic intellect
to read the secrets of your sect,
the marvelous delights
that your own hand indites
with loving letters in the eyes man craves.
With lovely, fluent words
you free the tongues of faithful slaves;
and oft (ah, strange and new,
Love's noble eloquence!),
oft in speech confused
and interrupted phrase
the heart makes known its sense
and seems to move more true
than if in learned and ornamented lays;
and silence still is wont to hear
a lover's words and lover's prayer.

O Love, let others read
Socratic argument,
in two fine eyes I'll learn that art's intent;
and let the rhyme be lost
from pens more wise than my
wild rhymes that coarsely cry,
which awkward hands on uncouth bark emboss.

Aminta

Intermedio Secondo

Sante leggi d'Amore e di Natura;
sacro laccio ch'ordio
fede sì pura di sì bel desio;
tenace nodo e forti e cari stami;
soave giogo e dilettevol salma
che fai l'umana compagnia gradita,
per cui regge due corpi un core, un'alma,
e per cui sempre si gioisca ed ami
sino a l'amara ed ultima partita;
gioia, conforto e pace
de la vita fugace;
del mal dolce ristoro ed alto oblio;
chi più di voi ne riconduce a Dio?

Interlude Two

Oh, holy laws of nature and of love,
pure faith it was that spread
and wove of fine desire the linking thread,
tenacious knot, the wool so dear and strong;
O yoke so soft, O burden sweet to bear,
you make companionship a great delight
through you one heart, one soul two bodies share,
through you we find our joy and love along
with it until the final, bitter night.
You — joy, comfort, peace
of lives, which fly and cease,
sweet solace for our ills, oblivion's stead —
who more than you can lead us to godhead?

Aminta

ATTO TERZO

SCENA PRIMA
TIRSI, CORO

TIRSI

Oh crudeltate estrema, oh ingrato core,
oh donna ingrata, oh tre fiate e quattro
ingratissimo sesso! E tu, Natura,
negligente maestra, perché solo
a le donne nel volto e in quel di fuori
ponesti quanto in loro è di gentile,
di mansueto e di cortese, e tutte
l'altre parti obliasti? Ahi, miserello,
forse ha se stesso ucciso; ei non appare;
io l'ho cerco e ricerco ormai tre ore
nel loco ov'io il lasciai e nei contorni:
né trovo lui né orme de' suoi passi.
Ahi, che s'è certo ucciso! Io vo' novella
chiederne a que' pastor che colà veggio.
Amici, avete visto Aminta, o inteso
novella di lui forse?

CORO

Tu mi pari
così turbato e qual cagion t'affanna?
Ond'è questo sudor, e questo ansare?
Havvi nulla di mal? fa che 'l sappiamo.

TIRSI

Temo del mal d'Aminta: avetel visto?

Act Three

Scene One
Tirsi and Chorus

Tirsi

Oh, cruelty extreme! Ungrateful heart!
Ungrateful girl! Oh, most ungrateful sex,
thrice thankless sex! And you, all negligent
instructress, Nature, why did you put all
there is of gentleness and courtesy
and sweetness in a woman's face and form
alone, and then forget to put them in
the parts within? Alas, unhappy man!
Perhaps he's killed himself; he's not appeared.
I've searched and searched again at least three hours
around the place I left him and nearby,
yet I've not found him, nor his footprints' mark.
Ah, what if he is dead! I want to ask
news of those shepherds that I see nearby.
Friends, have you seen Aminta, or heard news,
perhaps, of where he's gone?

Chorus

You seem to me
disturbed; what is it that upsets you so?
Whence comes your sweat and being out of breath?
Is something wrong with you? Oh, let us know.

Tirsi

I fear Aminta's hurt; have you seen him?

Coro

Noi visto non l'abbiam dapoi che teco,
buona pezza, partì; ma che ne temi?

Tirsi

Ch'egli non s'abbia ucciso di sua mano.

Coro

Ucciso di sua mano? or perché questo?
che ne stimi cagione?

Tirsi

Odio ed Amore.

Coro

Duo potenti inimici, insieme aggiunti,
che far non pònno? Ma parla più chiaro.

Tirsi

L'amar troppo una ninfa, e l'esser troppo
odiato da lei.

Coro

Deh, narra il tutto:
questo è luogo di passo, e forse intanto
alcun verrà che nova di lui rechi:
forse arrivar potrebbe anch'egli istesso.

Tirsi

Dirollo volontier, che non è giusto
che tanta ingratitudine e sì strana
senza l'infamia debita si resti.
Presentito avea Aminta (ed io fui, lasso,

CHORUS

We haven't seen him since some time ago
he left with you; but what is there to fear?

TIRSI

That he has killed himself with his own hand.

CHORUS

Killed by his hand? Oh, why would he do that?
What reason could there be?

TIRSI

Both Hate and Love.

CHORUS

Two potent enemies; together joined,
what can they not effect? But speak more clear.

TIRSI

He loved a nymph too much and was too much
by her despised.

CHORUS

Ah, tell us all you know.
This is a place of passage, and perhaps
someone will come meanwhile with news of him;
perhaps he'll come himself as we speak here.

TIRSI

I'll tell you willingly, for it's not just
ingratitude so great and strange should be
allowed to rest without a debt of shame.
Aminta had foreseen (and I, alas,

colui che riferì 'lo e che 'l condussi:
or me ne pento) che Silvia dovea
con Dafne ire a lavarsi ad una fonte.
Là dunque s'inviò dubbio ed incerto,
mosso non dal suo cor ma sol dal mio
stimolar importuno; e spesso in forse
fu ti tornar indietro, ed io 'l sospinsi,
pur mal suo grado, inanzi. Or quando omai
c'era il fonte vicino, ecco, sentiamo
un femminil lamento: e quasi a un tempo
Dafne veggiam, che battea palma a palma;
la qual, come ci vide, alzò la voce:
"Ah, correte," gridò. "Silvia è sforzata."
L'innamorato Aminta, che ciò intese,
si spiccò com'un pardo, ed io seguì 'lo;
ecco miriamo a un'arbore legata
la giovinetta ignuda come nacque,
ed a legarla fune era il suo crine:
il suo crine medesmo in mille nodi
a la pianta era avvolto; e 'l suo bel cinto,
che del sen virginal fu pria custode,
di quello stupro era ministro, ed ambe
le mani al duro tronco le stringea;
e la pianta medesma avea prestati
legami contra lei: ch'una ritorta
d'un pieghecole ramo avea a ciascuna
de le tenere gambe. A fronte a fronte
un satiro villan noi le vedemmo,
che di legarla pur allor finia.
Ella quanto potea faceva schermo:
ma che potuto avrebbe a lungo andare?
Aminta, con un dardo che tenea
ne la man destra, al satiro avventossi

was he who planned it all and led him there —
now I repent) that Silvia would come
with Dafne to the spring to wash herself.
Thus there he went, uncertain, full of doubt,
not moved by his own heart, but by my own
importunate demands; and oft in doubt
he wanted to return, but I urged on,
though much against his will. Then when at last
the spring was near, O Lord, we heard a cry,
a woman's cry, and at the selfsame time
we spotted Dafne beating both her hands.
As soon as she had seen us there, she yelled
and cried, "Ah, run, for Silvia is raped."
When amorous Aminta heard her word,
he, like a leopard, ran; I came behind.
And there we saw the sweet young girl tied to
a nearby tree, and nude as she was born;
her hair composed the cords that bound her there.
Her very hair, made in a thousand knots,
was wrapped around the tree. The lovely bands,
which guarded once her virgin breast from view,
became an agent of the rape, for both her hands
were fastened by it to the cruel trunk.
The plant itself participated too
in making ties to bind — a supple limb
became a bond, which tightly held each of
her tender legs. There face to face with her
we saw a satyr — villainous was he —
and he had finished binding her by then.
She tried to screen herself as best she could,
but in the long run what could she have done?
Aminta, with an arrow that he held
in his right hand, rushed at the satyr then,

come un leone, ed io fra tanto pieno
m'avea di sassi il grembo: onde fuggissi.
Come la fuga de l'altro concesse
spazio a lui di mirare, egli rivolse
i cupidi occhi in quelle membra belle,
che, come suole tremolare il latte
ne' giunchi, sì parean morbide e bianche.
E tutto 'l vidi sfavillar nel viso;
poscia accostossi pienamente a lei
tutto modesto, e disse: "O bella Silvia,
perdona a queste man, se troppo ardire
è l'appressarsi a le tue dolci membra,
perché necessità dura le sforza:
necessità di scioglier questi nodi;
né questa grazia che fortuna vuole
conceder loro, tuo mal grado sia."

CORO

Parole d'ammollir un cor di sasso.
Ma che rispose allor?

TIRSI

Nulla rispose,
ma disdegnosa e vergognosa a terra
chinava il viso, e 'l delicato seno
quanto poteta torcendosi celava.
Egli, fattosi innanzi, il biondo crine
cominciò a sviluppare, e disse in tanto:
"Già di nodi sì bei non era degno
così ruvido tronco: or, che vantaggio
hanno i servi d'Amor, se lor commune
è con le piante il prezioso laccio?
Pianta crudel, potesti quel bel crine,
offender tu, ch'a te feo tanto onore?"

just like a lion, and I meanwhile had filled
my arms with heavy stones: he saw and fled.
The satyr's flight allowed Aminta's eyes
to gaze upon her lovely form. He raised his eyes,
desiring, longing for those lovely limbs,
which seemed so soft and white, as milk is seen
to tremble gently in the rush-wove cups.
I saw these sweet sensations in his face.
Then softly he drew close to her and said,
all modestly, "O lovely Silvia,
forgive my hands, if they must dare too much
in drawing near the sweetness of your limbs,
for hard necessity moves them to act,
the need to loosen all these knots.
I hope the favor fortune grants them now
will not prove so displeasing to your heart."

CHORUS

Such words would soften hearts made out of stone.
But what did she reply?

TIRSI

She spoke no word;
disdainful and ashamed, she dropped her eyes
to earth and struggling sought to cover up
her smooth, soft breast, so far as possible.
Then he came up and started to untie
her golden hair, and all the while he said,
"Such rustic trunks were never worthy of
such knots so fair, for what advantage have
the slaves of Love, if such a precious snare
is shared in common with the common plants?
O cruel tree, how could you so offend
her tresses, which have honored you so much?"

Quinci con le sue man le man le sciolse
in modo tal, che parea che temesse
pur di toccarle, e desiasse insieme;
si chinò poi per islegarle i piedi:
ma come Silvia in libertà le mani
si vide, disse in atto dispettoso:
"Pastor, non mi toccar: son di Diana;
per me stessa saprò sciogliermi i piedi."

CORO

Or tanto orgoglio alberga in cor di ninfa?
Ah d'opra graziosa ingrato merto!

TIRSI

Ei si trasse in disparte riverente,
non alzando pur gli occhi per mirarla,
negando a se medesmo il suo piacere
per tôrre a lei fatica di negarlo.
Io, che m'era nascoso, e vedea il tutto
ed udia il tutto, allor fui per gridare;
pur mi ritenni. Or odi strana cosa.
Dopo molta fatica ella si sciolse;
e, sciolta a pena, senza dire 'A Dio,'
a fuggir cominciò com'una cerva;
e pur nulla cagione avea di tema,
che l'era noto il rispetto d'Aminta.

CORO

Perché dunque fuggissi?

TIRSI

A la sua fuga
volse l'obligo aver, non a l'altrui
modesto amore.

Then with his hands he freed her hand, yet in
a way that seemed to indicate he feared
that he might touch, yet that's what he desired.
He bent then that he might untie her feet,
but Silvia had seen her hands were free,
and spitefully she spoke to him and said,
"You shepherd, touch me not; I am Diane's.
I can untie my feet all by myself."

CHORUS

Can so much pride rest in the nymph's hard heart?
Ungracious answer to a gracious act!

TIRSI

He reverently drew himself aside
and did not dare to raise his eyes to her,
denying to himself his great desire
to save her from denying it herself.
And I, who hid, saw everything she did
and I heard all and was about to scream,
but I held back. Now hear a thing that's strange.
She freed herself though it was hard; once free
she did not pause to say good-bye to him,
but fled as fast as flees the running deer,
and not because she was afraid of him,
for well she knew Aminta's great respect.

CHORUS

Why did she run away?

TIRSI

Because she put her trust
in flight instead of in Aminta's love,
however chaste.

Coro

Ed in quest'anco è ingrata.
Ma che fe' 'l miserello allor? che disse?

Tirsi

No 'l so, ch'io, pien di mal talento, corsi
per arrivarla e ritenerla, e 'nvano,
ch'io la smarrii; e poi tornando dove
lasciai Aminta al fonte, no 'l trovai;
ma presago è il mio cor di qualche male.
So ch'egli era disposto di morire,
prima che ciò avvenisse.

Coro

È uso ed arte
di ciascun ch'ama minacciarsi morte:
ma rade volte poi segue l'effetto.

Tirsi

Dio faccia ch'ei non sia tra questi rari.

Coro

Non sarà, no.

Tirsi

Io voglio irmene a l'antro
del saggio Elpino: ivi, s'è vivo, forse
sarà ridotto, ove sovente suole
raddolcir gli amarissimi martiri
al dolce suon de la sampogna chiara,
ch'ad udir trae da gli alti monti i sassi,
e correr fa di puro latte i fiumi,
e stillar mele da le dure scorze.

CHORUS

In this she's thankless too.
But what did poor Aminta do? Or say?

TIRSI

I do not know, for angrily I ran
to catch her and to hold her back; in vain —
I lost her there. And then when I returned
to where I'd left Aminta by the spring,
I didn't find him. But my heart was filled
with ill foreboding: he had thought of death
before that happened.

CHORUS

It is usual
for one who loves to darkly threaten death;
infrequently the act will follow words.

TIRSI

God will that he is not among those few.

CHORUS

He shall not be.

TIRSI

I'm going to the cave
of wise Elpin'; if he's alive, perhaps
that's where he'll go, where often he was used
to sweeten so his bitterest laments
through sweet, soft sounds the pipes[27] drew clearly forth,
so that the sound would draw the rocks from hills
and make the rivers run with purest milk
and plumb the honey from the hardest bark.

Scena Seconda
Aminta, Dafne, Nerina

Aminta

Dispietata pietate
fu la tua veramente, o Dafne, allora
che ritenesti il dardo;
però che 'l mio morire
più amaro sarà, quanto più tardo.
Ed or perché m'avvolgi
per sì diverse strade e per sì varii
ragionamenti in vano? di che temi?
ch'io non m'uccida? Temi del mio bene.

Dafne

Non disperar, Aminta,
che, s'io lei ben conosco,
sola vergogna fu, non crudeltate,
quella che mosse Sivlia a fuggir via.

Aminta

Ohimè, che mia salute
sarebbe il disperare
poiché sol la speranza
è stata mia rovina; ed anco, ahi lasso,
tenta di germogliar dentr'al mio petto,
sol perché io viva: e quale è maggior male
de la vita d'un misero com'io?

Dafne

Vivi, misero, vivi
ne la miseria tua: e questo stato

Scene Two
Aminta, Dafne, and Nerina
(Aminta and Dafne, alone)

Aminta

Your pity truly was
dispiteous, O Dafne, when you held
my arrow back from me,
for death can only be
the bitterer the longer it's delayed.
Why are you leading me
through diverse ways and through such various,
vain arguments? What is it that you fear?
That I might kill myself? You fear my good.

Dafne

Aminta, don't despair.
For if I know her well,
not cruelty, but shame alone it was
made Silvia rush off and run away.

Aminta

Alas, if I despaired,
it would be for my good,
since hope alone's the cause
that led me to my ruin; and it, alas,
will try to grow within my breast again,
alone to make me live. And what ill's worse
than living miserably as I must live?

Dafne

Live, wretched man, live on
in your deep wretchedness and bear this state,

sopporta sol per divenir felice
quando che sia. Fia premio de la speme,
se vivendo e sperando ti mantieni,
quel che vedesti ne la bella ignuda.

AMINTA

Non pareva ad Amor e a mia fortuna
ch'a pien misero fossi, s'anco a pieno
non m'era dimostrato
quel che m'era negato.

NERINA

Dunque a me pur convien esser sinistra
còrnice d'amarissima novella!
Oh per mai sempre misero Montano,
qual animo fia 'l tuo quando udirai
de l'unica tua Silvia il duro caso?
Padre vecchio, orbo padre: ahi, non più padre!

DAFNE

Odo una mesta voce.

AMINTA

Io odo 'l nome
di Silvia, che gli orecchi e 'l cor mi fere;
ma chi è che la noma?

DAFNE

Ella è Nerina,
ninfa gentil che tanto a Cinzia è cara,
ch'ha sì begli occhi e così belle mani
e modi sì avvenenti e graziosi.

bear up alone, that one day you may be
a happier man. And may the prize of hope,
if living and hoping be your lot,
be what you saw in that fair, lovely nude.

AMINTA

It didn't seem to fortune and to Love
that I was sad enough, if just when she
was shown that way to me,
she was denied to me.

(*ENTER NERINA*)

NERINA

It's fallen, then, to me to be the grim
instructress of the bitterest news.
O dear Montano, ever miserable,
how will you bear it when you hear my words,
the hard case of your only Silvia?
Old man, bereft, ah, father never more!

DAFNE

I hear a grieving voice.

AMINTA

I hear the name
of Silvia, which wounds my ears and heart.
But who is it that speaks?

DAFNE

Nerina's she —
a gentle nymph who's dear to Cynthia[28] —
such lovely eyes she has, such lovely hands,
her ways are beautiful and filled with grace.

NERINA

E pur voglio che 'l sappi e che procuri
di ritrovar le reliquie infelici,
se nulla ve ne resta. Ahi Silvia, ahi dura
infelice tua sorte!

AMINTA

Ohimè, che fia? che costei dice?

NERINA

Dafne!

DAFNE

Che parli fra te stessa, e perché nomi
tu Silvia, e poi sospiri?

NERINA

Ahi, ch'a ragione
sospiro l'aspro caso!

AMINTA

Ahi, di qual caso
può ragionar costei? Io sento, io sento
che mi s'agghiaccia il core e mi si chiude
lo spirto. È viva?

DAFNE

Narra, qual aspro caso è quel che dici?

NERINA

O Dio, perché son io
la messaggiera? E pur convien narrarlo.
Venne Silvia al mio albergo ignuda: e quale
fosse l'occasion, saper la déi;

NERINA

I'd like someone to know, that they might try
and find again the sad remains, ah, if
a thing is left. Ah, Silvia! Ah, hard,
unhappy fate you've found!

AMINTA

Alas! What does she say?

NERINA

O Dafne, oh!

DAFNE

You're talking to yourself. Why call aloud
the name of Silvia and sigh?

NERINA

There's cause
to mourn the harsh event!

AMINTA

Ah! What event
can make her grieve that way? I feel, I feel
my heart turn all to ice and chill my soul.
Oh, tell me, does she live?

DAFNE

Tell us the harsh event of which you speak.

NERINA

O God, why is it I
who bears the news? And yet I must reply.
To my home Silvia came, nude, and what
the reason was I'm sure you know.

poi rivestita mi pregò che seco
ir volessi a la caccia che ordinata
era nel bosco ch'ha nome da l'elci.
Io la compiacqui: andammo: e ritrovammo
molte ninfe ridotte; ed indi a poco
ecco, di non so d'onde, un lupo sbuca,
grande fuor di misura, e da le labra
gocciolava una bava sanguinosa;
Silvia un quadrello adatta su la corda
d'un arco ch'io le diedi, e tira, e 'l coglie
a sommo 'l capo: ei si rinselva, ed ella,
vibrando un dardo, dentro 'l bosco il segue.

AMINTA

Oh dolente principio; ohimè, qual fine
già mi s'annuncia?

NERINA

Io con un altro dardo
séguo la traccia, ma lontana assai:
che più tarda mi mossi. Come fûro
dentro a la selva, più non la rividi:
ma pur per l'orme lor tanto m'avvolsi
che giunsi nel più folto e più deserto;
quivi il dardo di Silvia in terra scorsi,
né molto indi lontano un bianco velo
ch'io stessa le ravvolsi al crine; e, mentre
mi guardo intorno, vidi sette lupi
che leccavan di terra alquanto sangue
sparto intorno a cert'ossa affatto nude:
e fu mia sorte ch'io non fui veduta
da loro: tanto intenti erano al pasto;
tal che, piena di tema e di pietate,

When dressed, she begged that I should go with her,
for she was going to a hunt planned to
take place within the forest of the oaks.
And I agreed. We went and soon we found
so many nymphs who'd come. Almost at once
emerged, I cannot say from where, a wolf,
beyond all measure huge, and from his lips
there dripped a filthy, bloody slavering.
I gave a bow to Silvia, and she
set arrow to the cord and shot and struck
his skull, and he took to the woods, and she,
brandishing a dart, rushed after him.

AMINTA

Oh, sad beginning! Oh, alas, what end
I do perceive.

NERINA

I with another dart
did follow on their tracks, but far behind,
for I began too late. When they came to
the forest's edge, I didn't see her more,
but I still traced their footprints till I came
into the forest's deepest, darkest part.
I saw the dart of Silvia upon
the ground; not far away a white veil lay,
which I had wrapped around her hair. And while
I looked, there seven wolves I saw
who licked the bloody ground around some bones
spread round, which had been stripped quite bare of flesh.
It was my fate I was not seen by them,
they were so much intent upon their meal,
and, filled with fear and pity after that,

indietro ritornai; e questo è quanto
posso dirvi di Silvia: ed ecco 'l velo.

AMINTA

Poco pàrti aver detto? Oh velo, oh sangue,
oh Silvia, tu se' morta!

DAFNE

Oh miserello,
tramortito è d'affanno, e forse morto.

NERINA

Egli rispira pure: questo fia
un breve svenimento; ecco, riviene.

AMINTA

Dolor, che sì mi crucii,
che non m'uccidi, omai? tu sei pur lento!
Forse lasci l'officio a la mia mano.
Io son, io son contento
ch'ella prenda tal cura,
poi che tu la ricusi, o che non puoi.
Ohimè, se nulla manca
a la certezza omai,
e nulla manca al colmo
de la miseria mia,
che bado? che più aspetto? O Dafne, o Dafne,
a questo amaro fin tu mi salvasti,
a questo fine amaro?
Bello e dolce morir fu certo allora
che uccidere io mi volsi.
Tu me 'l negasti, e 'l Ciel, a cui parea
ch'io precorressi col morir la noia

I turned around. And this is all that I
can say of Silvia; and here's her veil.

AMINTA

Does what she said seem short? Oh, veil! Oh, blood!
O Silvia, you're dead!

DAFNE

O wretched man!
From grief he's fainted and perhaps he's dead.

NERINA

He's breathing still. I think that this will be
a fainting fit that's brief. Here, he revives.

AMINTA

O grief, which so torments,
why don't you kill me now? You are so slow!
Perhaps you've left the duty to my hand?
I am, I am content
that it should be the cause,
since you refuse to do it, or cannot.
Alas! If nothing lacks
to ascertain her death
and nothing lacks to make
my grief be greater still,
why care? Why wait? O Dafne, Dafne, why
preserve me for a bitter end like this,
for such a bitter end?
When I was set to kill myself before,
then dying was a sweet and lovely thing.
You held me back, and Heaven held me, for
it seemed I would forestall the pain it had

ch'apprestata m'avea.
Or che fatt'ha l'estremo
de la sua crudeltate,
ben soffrirà ch'io moia,
e tu soffrir lo déi.

DAFNE

Aspetta a la tua morte,
sin che 'l ver meglio intenda.

AMINTA

Ohimè, che vuoi ch'attenda?
Ohimè, che troppo ho atteso, e troppo inteso.

NERINA

Deh, foss'io stata muta!

AMINTA

Ninfa, dammi, ti prego
quel velo ch'è di lei
solo e misero avanzo,
sì ch'egli m'accompagne
per questo breve spazio
e di via e di vita che mi resta,
e con la sua presenza
accresca quel martire,
ch'è ben picciol martire
s'ho bisogno d'aiuto al mio morire.

NERINA

Debbo darlo o negarlo?
La cagion perché 'l chiedi
fa ch'io debba negarlo.

prepared for me with death.
Now that it's done its last
and utmost cruelty,
it sure must let me die,
and you must let me, too.

DAFNE

Delay your death until
the truth be better known.

AMINTA

Alas, why should I wait?
Alas, I've stayed too long and heard too much.

NERINA

Ah, I should have been mute!

AMINTA

I beg you, nymph, to let
me have that veil, which is
her sad and sole remains,
that it might come with me
down this short space and time
of light and life that still remains to me,
and though its presence here
shall spur my suffering,
such tiny suffering
may be the spur I need to hasten death.

NERINA

Ought I to grant or not?
The cause of your request
makes me deny your wish.

AMINTA

Crudel, sì picciol dono
mi nieghi al punto estremo?
E 'n questo anco maligno
mi si mostra il mio fato. Io cedo, io cedo:
a te si resti; e voi restate ancora,
ch'io vo per non tornare.

DAFNE

Aminta, aspetta, ascolta…
Ohimè, con quanta furia egli si parte!

NERINA

Egli va sì veloce,
che fia vano il seguirlo; ond'è pur meglio
ch'io segua il mio viaggio: e forse è meglio
ch'io taccia e nulla conti
al misero Montano.

CORO

Non bisogna la morte,
ch'a stringer nobil core
prima basta la fede, e poi l'amore.
Né quella che si cerca
è sì difficil fama
seguendo chi ben ama,
ch'amore è merce, e con amar si merca.
E cercando l'amor si trova spesso
gloria immortal appresso.

Act Three, Scene Two

AMINTA

Oh, harsh! You do deny
so small a gift, my last
request? My cruel fate
in this too shows itself. I yield, I yield;
you keep it then. And you also stay back.
I go and won't return.

DAFNE

Aminta, wait, and hear!
Alas, he left in such a maddened state!

NERINA

He goes so swiftly that
it would be vain to follow him. It's best
I go my way; perhaps it's best besides
that I be quiet, say naught
to poor Montano now.

CHORUS

We don't need death at all:
for heart to heart to bind
first faith we need, then love will come behind.
This search on which we dwell
is not so hard to say
if we see clear love's way,
for love is grace obtained by loving well.
And finding love, we also often find
immortal glory close behind.[29]

Intermedio Terzo

Divi noi siam, che ne 'l sereno eterno
fra celesti zaffiri e bei cristalli
meniam perpetui balli,
dove non è giamai state nè verno:
ed or grazia immortale, alta ventura
qua giù ne tragge, in questa bella imago
de 'l teatro de 'l mondo;
dove facciamo a tondo
un ballo nuovo e dilettoso e vago,
fra tanti lumi de la notte oscura
a la chiara armonia de 'l suono alterno.

Interlude Three

We are divine, and in eternal round
in our ensapphired blue and crystal halls,
we lead perpetual balls,
where never snow nor summer heat is found.
And now immortal grace and fortune bright
lead us down here to this fair image of
the theater of the world,
where we shall make awhirl
a new delightsome dance of joyous love,
amid the many torches in the night,
to clear, harmonious, otherworldly sound.

Atto Quarto

Scena Prima
Dafne, Silvia, Coro

Dafne

Ne porti il vento, con la ria novella
che s'era di te sparta, ogni tuo male
e presente e futuro. Tu sei viva
e sana, Dio lodato: ed io per morta
pur ora ti tenea: in tal maniera
m'avea Nerina il tuo caso dipinto.
Ahi, fosse stata muta, ed altri sordo!

Silvia

Certo 'l rischio fu grande, ed ella avea
giusta cagion di sospettarmi morta.

Dafne

Ma non giusta cagion avea di dirlo.
Or narra tu qual fosse 'l rischio, e come
tu lo fuggisti.

Silvia

Io, seguitando un lupo,
mi rinselvai nel più profondo bosco,
tanto ch'io ne perdei la traccia. Or, mentre
cerco di ritornare onde mi tolsi,
il vidi, e riconobbi a un stral che fitto
gli aveva di mia man press'un orecchio.
Il vidi con molt'altri intorno a un corpo
d'un animal ch'avea di fresco ucciso:
ma non distinsi ben la forma. Il lupo

Act Four

Scene One
Dafne, Silvia, and Chorus

Dafne

The wind was filled with evil news of you;
each sad misfortune, present and to come,
was spread upon the gale. You are alive
and safe, dear God be thanked; and I just now
held you for dead. In such a way the nymph
Nerina pictured your sad fate to me.
Had only she been mute, or he been deaf!

Silvia

The risk was surely great, and she had cause
enough to have suspected I was dead.

Dafne

But not just cause to say that it was so.
Now tell me why the risk was great and how
you got away.

Silvia

I, following a wolf,
within the forest's depth soon found myself,
so deep that I had lost the trace. Now while
I tried to turn to where I'd just come from,
I saw and knew him by an arrow that,
shot by my hand, was fixed behind his ear.
I saw him by the body of a beast
that had been freshly killed, with other wolves,
so that I couldn't see the form. The wolf

ferito, credo, mi conobbe, e 'ncontro
mi venne con la bocca sanguinosa.
Io l'aspettava ardita, e con la destra
vibrava un dardo. Tu sai ben s'io sono
maestra di ferire, e se mai soglio
far colpo in fallo. Or, quando il vidi tanto
vicin, che giusto spazio mi parea
a la percossa, lanciai un dardo, e 'n vano:
che, colpa di fortuna o pur mia colpa,
in vece sua colsi una pianta. Allora
più ingordo incontro ei mi venia: ed io
che 'l vidi sì vicin che stimai vano
l'uso de l'arco, non avendo altr'armi
a la fuga ricorsi. Io fuggo, ed egli
non resta di seguirmi. Or odi caso:
un vel, ch'aveva involto intorno al crine,
si spiegò in parte, e giva ventilando,
sì ch'ad un ramo avviluppossi. Io sento
che non so chi mi tien e mi ritarda.
Io, per la tema del morir, raddoppio
la forza al corso, e d'altra parte il ramo
non cede, e non mi lascia; al fin mi svolgo
del velo, e alquanto de' miei crini ancora
lascio svelti co 'l velo: e cotant'ali
m'impennò la paura ai piè fugaci,
ch'ei non mi giunse, e salva uscii del bosco.
Poi, tornando al mio albergo, io t'incontrai
tutta turbata, e mi stupii vedendo
stupirti al mio apparir.

DAFNE

Ohimè, tu vivi,
altri non già.

I wounded knew me — so I think — and came
against me then, blood dripping from its mouth.
Courageously I waited there and then
I raised my bow and shot. You know if I'm
a master shot, and if I ever miss
when I take aim. Thus when I saw him near
enough, so that the space looked right to me
to strike the blow, I shot — it was in vain.
For, whether fortune's fault or by my own,
instead of him I struck a tree. Then more
voraciously he came at me, and I
saw him so close I thought it was in vain
to use the bow. Not having other arms,
I took to flight. I ran and he did not
stop following behind. Now hear what chanced:
a veil that had been wrapped around my hair
unfurled in part and drifted on the wind
so that it caught upon a branch. I felt
some pull, which held me back and slowed my way.
But I, for fear of death, redoubled all
my efforts to escape, and yet the branch
would not give up and let me go. At last
I freed myself, but left some hair behind
tied to the veil. My fear became the wings
that feathered fleeing feet so that he did
not catch me, and I safely left the wood.
Then when returning to my home I met
you, all disturbed, and you surprised me when
you seemed astonished, seeing me.

DAFNE

You live —
alas, not he.

SILVIA

Che dici? ti rincresce
forse ch'io viva sia? M'odii tu tanto?

DAFNE

Mi piace di tua vita, ma mi duole
de l'altrui morte.

SILVIA

E di qual morte intendi?

DAFNE

De la morte d'Aminta.

SILVIA

Ahi, come è morto?

DAFNE

Il come non so dir, né so dir anco
s'è ver l'effetto: ma per certo il credo.

SILVIA

Ch'è ciò che tu mi dici? ed a chi rechi
la cagion di sua morte?

DAFNE

A la tua morte.

SILVIA

Io non t'intendo.

DAFNE

La dura novella
de la tua morte, ch'egli udì e credette,

SILVIA

What can you mean? Do you
regret that I'm alive? You hate me so?

DAFNE

I'm truly happy you're alive. I grieve
another's death.

SILVIA

And what death do you mean?

DAFNE

Aminta's death.

SILVIA

Ah! Is he dead? Ah, how?

DAFNE

I don't know how, nor am I even sure
if it is true, but I believe it true.

SILVIA

What are you telling me? And who has caused
his death?

DAFNE

The cause was you — your death.

SILVIA

I do not understand.

DAFNE

The grievous news
of your death, which he heard and thought was true,

avrà porto al meschino il laccio o 'l ferro
od altra cosa tal che l'avrà ucciso.

SILVIA

Vano il sospetto in te de la sua morte
sarà, come fu van de la mia morte;
ch'ognuno a suo poter salva la vita.

DAFNE

O Silvia, Silvia, tu non sai né credi
quanto 'l foco d'amor possa in un petto,
che petto sia di carne e non di pietra
com'è cotesto tuo: che, se creduto
l'avessi, avresti amato chi t'amava
più che le care pupille degli occhi,
più che lo spirto de la vita sua.
Il credo io ben, anzi l'ho visto e sollo:
il vidi, quando tu fuggisti, o fera
più che tigre crudel, ed in quel punto
ch'abbracciar lo dovevi, il vidi un dardo
rivolgere in se stesso, e quello al petto
premersi disperato, né pentirsi
poscia nel fatto, che le vesti ed anco
la pelle trapassossi, e nel suo sangue
lo tinse: e 'l ferro sarìa giunto a dentro,
e passato quel cor che tu passasti
più duramente, se non ch'io gli tenni
il braccio, e l'impedii ch'altro non fesse.
Ahi lassa, e forse quella breve piaga
solo una prova fu del suo furore
e de la disperata sua costanza,
e mostrò quella strada al ferro audace;
che correr poi dovea liberamente.

has led the wretched man to hang himself
or stab himself or die some other way.

SILVIA

The fear you have that he is dead will prove
quite false, as false as was my death's report,
for if he can, each man will save his life.

DAFNE

O Silvia, you neither think nor know
how in one's breast the fire of love can burn,
if it's a breast of flesh and not of stone,
as yours is made; because if you had known
you would have loved a man who loved you more
than he did love the pupils of his eyes,
more than the soul, which animates his life.
That I believe, for I have seen and know.
I saw him when you fled, you beast more harsh,
more cruel than the tiger, and when you
should have embraced him, I saw him direct
an arrow at himself and press it to
his breast most desperately, nor then regret
what he had done, although it passed clear through
his clothes and struck his flesh and stained it with
his very blood. He would have forced the point
still more and pierced the heart, which you had pierced
more harshly still, had I not held his arm
and thus impeded him from wounding more.
And now, alas! Perhaps that still small wound
was just a test, a trial for his mad acts
and of his desperate constancy, and showed
the way that the audacious iron could strike
when it could freely move without restraint.

Silvia

Oh, che mi narri?

Dafne

Il vidi poscia, allora
ch'intese l'amarissima novella
de la tua morte, tramortir d'affanno,
e poi partirsi furioso in fretta
per uccider se stesso: e s'avrà ucciso
veracemente.

Silvia

E ciò per fermo tieni?

Dafne

Io non v'ho dubbio.

Sivlia

Ohimè, tu no 'l seguisti
per impedirlo? Ohimè, cerchiamo, andiamo,
che poi ch'egli moria per la mia morte,
de' per la vita mia restar in vita.

Dafne

Io lo seguii, ma correa sì veloce
che mi sparì tosto dinanzi, e 'ndarno
poi mi girai per le sue orme. Or dove
vuoi tu cercar, se non n'hai traccia alcuna?

Silvia

Egli morrà, se no 'l troviamo, ahi lassa:
e sarà l'omicida ei di se stesso.

SILVIA

What are you saying. Oh!

DAFNE

I saw him then —
when he had heard the bitterest of news,
that of your death — fall senseless from his grief,
and afterwards rush out in furious haste
to kill himself. And now he will have done
it finally.

SILVIA

And so you think it's true?

DAFNE

I have no doubt.

SILVIA

Alas! You did not run
to stop him? Run, let's search him out. Let's go.
For since he would have died if I were dead,
my living should restore his will to live.

DAFNE

I followed him, but he so swiftly ran
that soon he disappeared, and I in vain
ran where his footprints led. Now where would you
begin the search, if there's no path to trace?

SILVIA

He'll die if we don't find him, ah, alas!
And his own hand shall wield the killing blow.

DAFNE

Crudel, forse t'incresce ch'a te tolga
la gloria di quest'atto? esser tu dunque
l'omicida vorresti? e non ti pare
che la sua cruda morte esser debb'opra
d'altri che di tua mano? Or ti consola,
che, comunque egli muoia, per te muore,
e tu sei che l'uccidi.

SILVIA

Ohimè, che tu m'accori, e quel cordoglio
ch'io sento del suo caso inacerbisce
con l'acerba memoria
de la mia crudeltate,
ch'io chiamava onestate; e ben fu tale:
ma fu troppo severa e rigorosa:
or me n'accorgo e pento.

DAFNE

Oh, quel ch'io odo!
Tu sei pietosa, tu, tu senti al core
spirto alcun di pietate? oh che vegg'io?
tu piangi, tu superba? Oh maraviglia!
Che pianto è questo tuo? pianto d'amore?

SILVIA

Pianto d'amor non già, ma di pietate.

DAFNE

La pietà messaggiera è de l'amore,
come 'l lampo del tuono.

DAFNE

O cruel girl, do you regret that he
will take the glory of his act from you?
Then you would like to be the murderer?
It doesn't seem to you his cruel death
should come from any hand but yours? Be still,
however he may die, he dies for you,
and you have murdered him.

SILVIA

Alas, you make me sad! And all the grief
I feel for his sad fate grows bitterer
with bitter memories
of all my cruel ways,
which I called chastity, and that it was,
but it was too severe and rigorous.
I know it now and grieve.

DAFNE

What do I hear?
You pity, you? You feel within your heart
some sense of pity? Oh, what do I see?
You're weeping, you? Proud girl? Oh, marvelous!
What is this tear of yours? A tear of love?

SILVIA

A tear of pity, not a tear of love.

DAFNE

Compassion is the messenger of love
as lightning heralds thunder.

CORO

Anzi sovente
quando egli vuol ne' petti virginelli
occulto entare, onde fu prima escluso
da severa onestà, l'abito prende,
prende l'aspetto de la sua ministra
e sua nuncia, pietate; e con tai larve
le semplici ingannando, è dentro accolto.

DAFNE

Questo è pianto d'amor: che troppo abonda.
Tu taci? ami tu, Silvia? ami, ma in vano.
Oh potenza d'Amor, giusto castigo
manda sovra costei. Misero Aminta!
Tu, in guisa d'ape che ferendo muore
e ne le piaghe altrui lascia la vita,
con la tua morte hai pur trafitto al fine
quel duro cor che non potesti mai
punger vivendo. Or, se tu, spirto errante,
sì come io credo, e de le membra ignudo,
qui intanto sei, mira il suo pianto, e godi.
Amante in vita, amato in morte: e s'era
tuo destin che tu fossi in morte amato,
e se questa crudel volea l'amore
venderti sol con prezzo così caro,
desti quel prezzo tu ch'ella richiese,
e l'amor suo col tuo morir comprasti.

CORO

Caro prezzo a chi 'l diede; a chi 'l riceve
prezzo inutile, e infame.

Chorus

Often when
he wants to enter secretly the breasts
of virgin maidens where he was kept out
by stern, harsh chastity, he wears the clothes
and takes the aspect of his messenger
and minister, compassion: with such tricks,
beguiling innocents, he's welcomed in.

Dafne

This is a tear of love, so fast they fall.
You're quiet? You love him, Silvia? In vain.
O mighty power of Love, just punishment
you send on her. Aminta, wretched man!
Just like the bee, which, stinging, dies and in
the wounds of others leaves its life, are you.
By dying you have even pierced the depth
of that hard heart which you could never sting
alive.[30] O wand'ring spirit, if you are
around this spot, with death denuded limbs,
as I believe, observe her tears! Enjoy!
Loving in life, you are beloved in death.
It was your fate to be beloved in death,
and if this cruel girl did want to sell
her love to you at such a precious price,
you met the price that she required of you
and bought her love by paying with your life.

Chorus

High price for him who paid; a useless price,
and infamous for who received.

SILVIA

Oh potess'io
con l'amor mio comprar la vita sua;
s'egli è pur morto!

DAFNE

O tardi saggia, e tardi
pietosa, quando ciò nulla rileva!

SCENA SECONDA
ERGASTO, CORO, SILVIA, DAFNE

ERGASTO

Io ho sì pieno il petto di pietate
e sì pieno d'orror, che non rimiro
né odo alcuna cosa, ond'io mi volga,
la qual non mi spaventi e non m'affanni.

CORO

Or ch'apporta costui,
ch'è sì turbato in vista ed in favella?

ERGASTO

Porto l'aspra novella
de la morte d'Aminta.

SILVIA

Ohimè, che dice?

ERGASTO

Il più nobil pastor di queste selve,
che fu così gentil, così leggiadro,

SILVIA

Oh, could
I buy his life by giving him my love,
should he be dead!

DAFNE

Oh, late you're wise and late
you're pitying, for now it matters not.

SCENE TWO
ERGASTO, SILVIA, DAFNE, AND CHORUS

ERGASTO[31]

I've filled my heart with such compassion, and
such horror that I cannot see or hear
a single thing, wherever I may turn,
that doesn't frighten me or cause me grief.

CHORUS

What is it that he bears
that he is so disturbed in face and speech?

ERGASTO

I bring the bitter news:
Aminta's dead.

SILVIA

Alas, what do you mean?

ERGASTO

The noblest shepherd of these forest paths,
who was so kind, so handsome, and so dear

così caro a le ninfe ed a le Muse,
ed è morto fanciullo, ahi, di che morte!

Coro

Contane, prego, il tutto, acciò che teco
pianger possiam la sua sciagura e nostra.

Silvia

Ohimè, ch'io non ardisco
appressarmi ad udire
quel ch'è pur forza udire. Empio mio core,
mio duro alpestre core,
di che, di che paventi?
Vattene incontra pure
a quei coltei pungenti
che costui porta ne la lingua, e quivi
mostra la tua fierezza.
Pastore, io vengo a parte
di quel dolor che tu prometti altrui;
che a me ben si conviene
più forse che non pensi; ed io 'l ricevo
come dovuta cosa. Or tu di lui
non mi sii dunque scarso.

Ergasto

Ninfa, io ti credo bene,
ch'io sentii quel meschino in su la morte
finir la vita sua
co 'l chiamar il tuo nome.

Dafne

Ora comincia omai
questa dolente istoria.

to all the nymphs and to the Muses here;
and he is dead, so young. A grievous death!

CHORUS

I pray you, tell us all that we may weep
with you, his great misfortune and our own.

SILVIA

Alas, I do not dare
to draw nearby to hear
what still I'm forced to hear! Impious heart,
my hard and stony heart,
why, why are you afraid?
Go bravely on before
the sharp and piercing knives
he bears upon his tongue, and there display
your self respect and pride.
Shepherd, I come to share
in all that grief you promise for the rest,
because such grief is fitting more for me
than you perhaps might think, and I receive
it as my rightful due. Then do not stint
in what you say of him.

ERGASTO

O nymph, I think you're right,
for I just heard that wretch whose death I tell
conclude his life on earth
by calling out your name.

DAFNE

Come on, begin at last
to tell your grievous tale.

Ergasto

Io era a mezzo 'l colle, ove avea tese
certe mie reti, quando assai vicino
vidi passar Aminta, in volto e in atti
troppo mutato da quel ch'ei soleva,
troppo turbato e scuro. Io corsi, e corsi
tanto che 'l giunsi, e lo fermai: ed egli
mi disse: "Ergasto, io vo' che tu mi faccia
un gran piacer: quest'è, che tu ne venga
meco per testimonio d'un mio fatto;
ma pria voglio da te che tu mi leghi
di stretto giuramento la tua fede
di startene in disparte e non por mano
per impedirmi in quel che son per fare."
Io (chi pensato avria caso sì strano,
né sì pazzo furor?), com'egli volse,
feci scongiuri orribili, chiamando
e Pane e Pale e Priapo e Pomona,
ed Ecate notturna. Indi si mosse,
e mi condusse ov'è scosceso il colle,
e giù per balzi e per dirupi incolti
strada non già, che non v'è strada alcuna,
ma cala un precipizio in una valle.
Qui ci fermammo. Io, rimirando a basso,
tutto sentii raccapricciarmi, e 'ndietro
tosto mi trassi; ed egli un cotal poco
parve ridesse, e serenossi in viso:
onde quell'atto più rassicurommi.
Indi parlommi sì: "Fa che tu conti
a le ninfe e ai pastor ciò che vedrai."
Poi disse, in giù guardando:
"Se presti a mio volere
così aver io potessi

Act Four, Scene Two

ERGASTO

Up in the hills I was, where I had fixed
some nets of mine, when I saw pass nearby
Aminta, and in all his acts and looks
much changed from that which he had been before,
so overly disturbed and dark. I rose
and ran, and when I caught him up he stopped
and spoke: "Ergasto, would you do for me
what I request? That is, that you will come
with me as witness of an act I plan,
but first I wish that you would bind your faith
to me by strictest oath that man can make
to stand apart from me and not raise hand
to hold me back from that which I must do."
And I (who would have thought a case so strange
and full of crazy madness?), as he wished,
made horrible entreaties, calling on
Pomona, Pallas, Pan, Priapus, and
Hecate of the night.[32] Then he moved off
and led me on to where the hills are rough
and up through cliffs and crags no man has tilled:
the road ran out. There was no road that high,
but precipices plunged to vales below.
And there we stopped. I looked below and felt
myself quite terrified and quickly drew
myself away; but he, he seemed to laugh
a bit, and on his face — serenity.
By this mood I was reassured somewhat.
And then he spoke to me: "See that you tell
the nymphs and shepherds what you see me do."
Then looking down, he said,
"If I could have my way,
then I would have the maws

la gola e i denti degli avidi lupi
com'ho questi dirupi,
sol vorrei far la morte
che fece la mia vita:
vorrei che queste mie membra meschine
sì fosser lacerate,
ohimè, come già foro
quelle sue delicate.
Poi che non posso, e 'l Cielo
dinega al mio desire
gli animali voraci,
che ben verriano a tempo, io prender voglio
altra strada al morire:
prenderò quella via
che, se non la devuta,
almen fia la più breve.
Silvia, io ti seguo, io vengo
a farti compagnia,
se non la sdegnerai:
e morirei contento,
s'io fossi certo almeno
che 'l mio venirti dietro
turbar non ti dovesse,
e che fosse finita
l'ira tua con la vita.
Silvia, io ti seguo, io vengo." Così detto,
precipitossi d'alto
co 'l capo in giuso: ed io restai di ghiaccio.

DAFNE

Misero Aminta!

SILVIA

Ohimè!

and teeth of eager, greedy wolves instead
of rocks such as I have.
I'd to have a death
like that which took my life[33];
if only these, my wretched limbs could be
as torn and ripped apart,
as her limbs, ever delicate,
alas, were torn before.
But since I cannot and
the gods deny my wish
for hungry animals
whose coming I would welcome, I will take
another road to death.
I'll take that way, which if
it's not what it should be,
at least it will be short.
O Silvia, I follow you. I come
as your companion, friend,
if you will not disdain.
And I shall die, content,
if I could just be sure
my coming now, behind,
will not disturb your peace,
and that your anger will
be finished with your life.
O Silvia, I follow you, I come."
He spoke and threw himself
straight down headfirst, and I remained like ice.

DAFNE

Aminta, wretched man!

SILVIA

Alas!

CORO

Perché non l'impedisti?
Forse ti fu ritegno a ritenerlo
il fatto giuramento?

ERGASTO

Questo no, che sprezzando i giuramenti,
vani forse in tal caso,
quand'io m'accorsi del suo pazzo ed empio
proponimento, con la man vi corsi,
e, come volse la sua dura sorte,
lo presi in questa fascia di zendado
che lo cingeva; la qual, non potendo
l'impeto e 'l peso sostener del corpo,
che s'era tutto abandonato, in mano
spezzata mi rimase.

CORO

E che divenne
de l'infelice corpo?

ERGASTO

Io no 'l so dire:
ch'era sì pien d'orrore e di pietate,
che non mi diede il cor di rimirarvi,
per non vederlo in pezzi.

CORO

Oh strano caso!

SILVIA

Ohimè, ben son di sasso,
poi che questa novella non m'uccide.

CHORUS

You didn't stop his act?
Perhaps the oath you swore was a restraint
from holding him?

ERGASTO

Not so, for I disdained the oaths I made —
in such a case they're vain.
When I became aware his thought was mad
and impious, I ran with hand outstretched
and as he leapt to carry out his fate,
I seized him by the soft and silken band
that circled him, but it could not sustain
his force of fall and body's heaviness,
and when he fell it stayed within my hand,
in fragments, pieces, bits.

CHORUS

And what became
of his unhappy corpse?

ERGASTO

I do not know.
I was so horrified and piteous
I didn't have the heart to stay up there
and see his body smashed.

CHORUS

Oh, strange event!

SILVIA

Alas! I'm made of stone,
since news like this does not bring on my death.

Ahi, se la falsa morte
di chi tanto l'odiava
a lui tolse la vita,
ben sarebbe ragione
che la verace morte
di chi tanto m'amava
togliesse a me la vita;
e vo' che la mi tolga,
se non potrà co 'l duol, almen co 'l ferro,
o pur con questa fascia,
che non senza cagione
non seguì le ruine
del suo dolce signore,
ma restò sol per fare in me vendetta
de l'empio mio rigore
e del suo amaro fine.
Cinto infelice, cinto
di signore più infelice,
non ti spiaccia restare
in sì odioso albergo,
che tu vi resti sol per instrumento
di vendetta e di pena.
Dovea certo, io dovea
esser compagna al mondo
de l'infelice Aminta.
Poscia ch'allor non volsi,
sarò per opra tua
sua compagna a l'Inferno.

CORO

Consolati, meschina,
che questo è di fortuna e non tua colpa.

Ah! If the wrong-told death
of she who hated him
did steal his life away,
it surely would be right
if this true tale of death
in one who loved me so
would take my life from me.
I'd have it take my life,
and if grief cannot kill, a knife will do,
or better yet this band,
which followed not the ruin
its sweet lord took himself,
and not without a cause,
for it remains to wreak his vengeance on
my gross severity
and for his bitter end.
So sad a band, a band
that bound a lord so sad,
aren't you displeased to stay
in such a hateful place,
when you remain alone as instrument
of vengeance and of pain?
I should, I should have been
companion in the world
of poor Aminta, but
since that was not my wish,
I shall through you become
companion to his hell.

CHORUS

O wretched girl, take heart,
for this is fortune's blow, and not from you.

Silvia

Pastor, di che piangete?
Se piangete il mio affanno,
io non merto pietate,
che non la seppi usare:
se piangete il morire
del misero innocente,
questo è picciolo segno
a sì alta cagione. E tu rasciuga,
Dafne, queste tue lagrime, per Dio.
Se cagion ne son io,
ben ti voglio pregare,
non per pietà di me, ma per pietate
di chi degno ne fue,
che m'aiuti a cercare
l'infelici sue membra, e a sepelirle.
Questo sol mi ritiene
ch'or ora non m'uccida:
pagar vo' questo ufficio,
poi ch'altro non m'avanza,
a l'amor ch'ei portommi:
e se bene quest'empia
mano contaminare
potesse la pietà de l'opra, pure
so che gli sarà cara
l'opra di questa mano;
che so certo ch'ei m'ama,
come mostrò morendo.

Dafne

Son contenta aiutarti in questo ufficio:
ma tu già non pensare
d'aver poscia a morire.

SILVIA

O shepherds, why lament?
If you cry for my grief,
no pity merit I,
for I had none myself.
If you cry for the death
of that poor innocent,
it is small token of
a cause as great as that. And you must dry
your tears, O Dafne, in the name of God.
If I'm the cause of them,
I beg that you will give
me help to find that man's unhappy limbs
and bury them, not as
you pity me but for
the sake of one whose life deserves your tears.
This only keeps me back
from killing myself now:
I wish to do this task,
since that is all that I
can offer to his love.
And if this impious hand
might stain the peaceful, mild
compassion of the act, yet still I know
that my hand's act will be
an act of love to him,
for I am sure he loves
me, as he, dying, showed.

DAFNE

I am content to help you with this deed,
but you must never think
of dying afterwards.

SILVIA

Sin qui vissi a me stessa,
a la mia feritate: or, quel ch'avanza,
viver voglio ad Aminta:
e, se non posso a lui,
viverò al freddo suo
cadavero infelice.
Tanto, e non più, mi lice
restar nel mondo, e poi finir a un punto
e l'essequie e la vita.
Pastor, ma quale strada
ci conduce a la valle ove il dirupo
va a terminare?

ERGASTO

Questa vi conduce;
e quinci poco spazio ella è lontana.

DAFNE

Andiam, che verrò teco e guiderotti;
che ben rammento il luogo.

SILVIA

A Dio, pastori;
piagge, a Dio; a Dio, selve; e fiumi, a Dio.

ERGASTO

Costei parla di modo, che dimostra
d'essere disposta a l'ultima partita.

CORO

Ciò che morte rallenta, Amor, restringi,
amico tu di pace, ella di guerra,

SILVIA

I lived for cruelty,
for self 'til now; for what is left, I wish
to live for him alone,
and if I cannot live
with him, I'll live nearby
his cold, unhappy corpse.
This much — no more — allows
that I remain alive, and then I'll end
lamenting and my life.
O shepherd, can you show
the road that leads out to the valley floor
from which those cliffs rise up?

ERGASTO

This takes you there,
and it is not so far away from here.

DAFNE

Let's go, for I shall come and lead the way,
for I recall the place.

SILVIA

Farewell, kind friends.
O hills, farewell. Farewell, you woods and streams.

ERGASTO

She speaks in such a way that shows that she
is leaving for the last and final time.

CHORUS

What death destroys, you, Love, make anew;
the friend of peace are you, and she of wars,

e del suo trionfar trionfi e regni;
e mentre due bell'alme annodi e cingi,
così rendi sembiante al ciel la terra,
che d'abitarla tu non fuggi o sdegni.
Non so ire là su: gli umani ingegni
tu placidi ne rendi, e l'odio interno
sgombri, signor, da' mansueti cori,
sgombri mille furori;
e quasi fai col tuo valor superno
de le cose mortali un giro eterno.

but you, on her triumph, triumph and reign.
And when you bind and mold one soul from two,
you strew on earth the semblance of the stars,
for to abide with us you don't disdain.
Above no anger is: you make men sane
in understanding, calm, and strike entire,
O Lord, from gentle hearts all trace of hate,
all rage eliminate;
as if you, by supernal worth, inspire
mere man to soar in an immortal gyre.[34]

Aminta

Intermedio Quarto

Itene, o mesti amanti, o donne liete,
ch' tempo ormai di placida quiete:
itene co 'l silenzio, ite co 'l sonno,
mentre versa papaveri e viole
la Notte, e fugge il Sole.
E se i pensieri in voi dormir non ponno,
sian gli affanni amorosi
in vece a voi di placidi riposi;
né miri il vostro pianto aurora o luna.
Il gran Pan vi licenzia: omai tacete,
alme serve d'Amor, fide e secrete.

Interlude Four

Then go, sad lovers, happy ladies, go,
for now's the time that placid quiet will flow.
So go with silence, go with restful sleep,
while night pours poppies down and violets,
and sunlight sinks and sets.
If troubling thoughts should steal your rest and keep
you up, may they attest
to am'rous pain instead of placid rest;
nor dawn nor moon be witness of your tears.
Great Pan bids you farewell; now show
your silence, faithful slaves of Love, and go.

Atto Quinto

Scena Prima
Elpino, Coro

Elpino

Veramente la legge con che Amore
il suo imperio governa eternamente
non è dura, né obliqua; e l'opre sue,
piene di providenza e di mistero,
altri a torto condanna. Oh con quant'arte,
e per che ignote strade egli conduce
l'uom ad esser beato, e fra le gioie
del suo amoroso paradiso il pone,
quando ei più crede al fondo esser de' mali!
Eccvo, precipitando, Aminta ascende
al colmo, al sommo d'ogni contentezza.
Oh fortunato Aminta, oh te felice
tanto più, quanto misero più fosti!
Or co 'l tuo essempio a me lice sperare,
quando che sia, che quella bella ed empia,
che sotto il riso di pietà ricopre
il mortal ferro di sua feritate,
sani le piaghe mie con pietà vera,
che con finta pietate al cor mi fece.

Coro

Quel che viene è il saggio Elpino, e parla
così d'Aminta come vivo ei fosse,
chiamandolo felice e fortunato:
dura condizione degli amanti!
Forse egli stima fortunato amante
chi muore, e morto al fin pietà ritrova

Act Five

Scene One
Elpino and Chorus

Elpino

Oh certainly the law of Love, with which
eternally he governs all his reign
is nether harsh nor hard, and all his works
are full of providence and mystery,
which wrongly some condemn. Oh, with what art
and through what unknown streets he leads his man
to blessedness, and places him amid
the joys of his am'rous paradise
when he is sure he's sunk amid his ills!
See here, Aminta, hurled down to the ground,
who gains the heights, the summit of content.
O fortunate Aminta! Joyous,
oh, so much more than you were sad before!
Your situation gives me leave to hope
a time will come when one so fair as false,
who in a laugh of pity covers up
the fatal knife of her harsh cruelty,
will heal with true compassion all the wounds
she made with false compassion in my heart.[35]

Chorus

The wise Elpino's he who comes and speaks
of poor Aminta as if he still lived,
and calling him both fortunate and glad.
Oh, hard conditions lovers must endure!
Perhaps he holds the lover fortunate
who dies, and, dead, finds pity at the end

nel cor de la sua ninfa; e questo chiama
paradiso d'Amore, e questo spera.
Di che lieve mercé l'alato Dio
i suoi servi contenta! Elpin, tu dunque
in sì misero stato sei, che chiami
fortunata la morte miserabile
de l'infelice Aminta? e un simil fine
sortir vorresti?

ELPINO

Amici, state allegri,
che falso è quel romor che a voi pervenne
de la sua morte.

CORO

Oh che ci narri, e quanto
ci racconsoli! E non è dunque il vero
che si precipitasse?

ELPINO

Anzi è pur vero,
ma fu felice il precipizio: e sotto
una dolente imagine di morte
gli recò vita e gioia. Egli or si giace
nel seno accolto de l'amata ninfa,
quanto spietata già, tanto or pietosa;
e le rasciuga da' begli occhi il pianto
con la sua bocca. Io a trovar ne vado
Montano, di lei padre, ed a condurlo
colà dov'essi stanno; e solo il suo
volere è quel che manca, e che prolunga
il concorde voler d'ambidue loro.

within the nymph's proud heart; and this he calls
a paradise of Love, and hopes for this.
With what an easy grace the winged god
contents his slaves! Elpino, are you then
in such a wretched state that you would call
the miserable, unhappy death of poor
Aminta fortunate? And would you choose
a similar demise?

ELPINO

O friends, be glad,
because the rumor of his death, which came
to you, was false.

CHORUS

What do you say! Oh how
you offer us relief! Then was it false,
he hurled himself headlong?

ELPINO

No, it was true,
but still his fall was fortunate, and from
the effigy of death, so full of grief,
he's found both life and joy. And now he lies
upon the breast of one he loved — that nymph
as full of pity now as pitiless
she was; and with his lips he dries the tears
upon her eyes. I'm going now to find
Montano, her good father, and to lead
him where they are. For all that's lacking now
is that he bless them, and thereby extend
the blessing that they feel between them both.

Coro

Pari è l'età, la gentilezza è pari,
e concorde il desio: e 'l buon Montano
vago è d'aver nipoti e di munire
di sì dolce presidio la vecchiaia:
sì che farà del lor voler il suo.
Ma tu, deh, Elpin, narra qual Dio, qual sorte
nel periglioso precipizio Aminta
abbia salvato.

Elpino

Io son contento: udite,
udite quel che con quest'occhi ho visto.
Io era anzi il mio speco, che si giace
presso la valle, e quasi a piè del colle,
dove la costa face di sé grembo:
quivi con Tirsi ragionando andava
pur di colei che ne l'istessa rete
lui prima e me dapoi ravvolse e strinse,
e proponendo a la sua fuga, al suo
libero stato, il mio dolce servigio:
quando ci trasse gli occhi ad alto un grido:
e 'l veder rovinar un uom dal sommo,
e 'l vederlo cader sovra una macchia,
fu tutto un punto. Sporgea fuor del colle,
poco di sopra a noi, d'erbe e di spini
e d'altri rami strettamente giunti
e quasi in un tessuti, un fascio grande.
Quivi, prima che urtasse in altro luogo,
a cader venne: e bench'egli co 'l peso
lo sfondasse, e più in giuso indi cadesse,
quasi su' nostri piedi, quel ritegno
tanto d'impeto tolse a la caduta,

CHORUS

Their age is equal, and their gentleness[36]
and their desire, and good Montano wants
to have some little ones to make secure
old age, for they are such a sweet defense,
and so he'll bless them with conjoined will.
But you, Elpino, tell what god, what fate
has saved Aminta from the dangerous
ravine.

ELPINO

I am content. Now hear my words,
now hear what I have seen with my own eyes.
I stood before my cave, which lies nearby
the valley, almost at the hillside's slope,
which makes itself a kind of lap or breast.
I wandered, reasoning, with Tirsi at
that spot, of her, and of the selfsame net
that first held him and then had captured me,
his flight from her, his freedom giving me
the sweetness of my servitude to her.[37]
Then all at once a cry raised up our eyes.
We saw a person tumbling from above,
and falling down into a bush. It took
a moment's time. There jutted outward from
the hill, a bit above us, made of grass
and thorny spines and branches closely joined,
a thicket, great, and like a fabric woven.
And it was there that first he fell before
he struck another spot; and though his weight
made him break through and tumble farther down,
now almost to our feet, that soft restraint
took so much impetus from his swift fall,

ch'ella non fu mortal; fu nondimeno
grave così, ch'ei giacque un'ora e piue
stordito affatto e di se stesso fuori.
Noi muti di pietate e di stupore
restammo a lo spettacolo improviso,
riconoscendo lui; ma conoscendo
ch'egli morto non era, e che non era
per morir forse, mitighiam l'affanno.
Allor Tirsi mi diè notizia intiera
de' suoi secreti ed angosciosi amori.
Ma, mentre procuriam di ravvivarlo
con diversi argomenti, avendo in tanto
già mandato a chiamar Alfesibeo
a cui Febo insegnò la medica arte
allor che diede a me la cetra e 'l plettro,
sopragiunsero insieme Dafne e Silvia:
che, come intesi poi, givan cercando
quel corpo che credean di vita privo.
Ma, come Silvia il riconobbe, e vide
le belle guancie tenere d'Aminta
iscolorite in sì leggiadri modi
che viola non è che impallidisca
sì dolcemente, e lui languir sì fatto
che parea già negli ultimi sospiri
essalar l'alma: in guisa di baccante
gridando e percotendosi il bel petto,
lasciò cadersi in su 'l giacente corpo:
e giunse viso a viso e bocca a bocca.

CORO

Or non ritenne adunque la vergogna
lei, ch'è tanto severa e schiva tanto?

it wasn't fatal. Nonetheless it was
so serious he lay an hour and more
quite deaf and quite unconscious to the world.
Struck down by pity and amazement, we
stood by and watched the unexpected sight,
and recognized his face. But knowing that
he was not dead, and that he was not just
about to die, alleviated pain.
Then Tirsi gave me all the news about
his secrets and the anguish of his love.
But while we were attempting to revive
him in our various ways — already we
had sent to summon Alphesibius,
to whom great Phoebus gave the healing arts
when he gave me the plectrum and the lyre[38] —
Silvia and Dafne came upon
us. They, as then I heard, had gone to find
his body, which they thought deprived of life.
When Silvia had recognized him and
had seen Aminta's tender, lovely cheeks,
deprived so charmingly of coloring —
no violet grows so gently pale and wan
as that — in such a way he seemed to pine
away, and in his sighs already breathe
away his soul, as if a bacchant she'd
become, she screamed and beat her lovely breast,
and fell upon his body lying there
and brought them face to face and mouth to mouth.

CHORUS

And she retained no bit of shame at all —
she who is so severe and is so shy?

ELPINO

La vergogna ritien debile amore:
ma debil freno è di potente amore.
Poi, sì come negli occhi avesse un fonte,
inaffiar cominciò co 'l pianto suo
il colui freddo viso, e fu quell'acqua
di cotanta virtù, ch'egli rivenne:
e gli occhi aprendo, un doloroso ohimè
spinse dal petto interno;
*ma quell'*ohimè, *ch'amaro*
così dal cor partissi,
s'incontrò ne lo spirto
de la sua cara Silvia, e fu raccolto
da la soave bocca: e tutto quivi
subito raddolcissi.
Or chi potrebbe dir come in quel punto
rimanessero entrambi, fatto certo
ciascun de l'altrui vita, e fatto certo
Aminta de l'amor de la sua ninfa,
e vistosi con lei congiunto e stretto?
Chi è servo d'Amor, per sé lo stimi.
Ma non si può stimar, non che ridire.

CORO

Aminta, è sano sì, ch'egli sia fuori
del rischio de la vita?

ELPINO

Aminta è sano,
se non ch'alquanto pur graffiato ha 'l viso,
ed alquanto dirotta la persona;
ma sarà nulla, ed ei per nulla il tiene.
Felice lui, che sì gran segno ha dato

ELPINO

It's true that shame restrains a love that's weak,
but it's a weak restraint for potent love.
As if she had a fountain in her eyes,
she then began to bathe his frigid face
with all her tears: that water was the thing,
filled with rare virtues, that revived him, and
on opening his eyes, a sad "alas"
escaped and shook his chest.
But that "alas," which left
his heart so bitterly,
was met within the soul
of his dear Silvia, and gathered up
by her sweet lips, and there all suddenly
all grieving was assuaged.
Now who could say how in that moment they
remained together, reassuring each
that they were still alive, assuring too
Aminta of the love his nymph now felt,
and so conjoined lay and loved as one?
Who serves great Love will know it for himself.
But one who doesn't know, much less can tell.

CHORUS

Then is Aminta well enough that he
is out of danger?

ELPINO

Yes, Aminta's well,
although his face is scratched and torn a bit,
and elsewhere too his body might be bruised,
but it is nothing and he holds it naught.
Oh, happy he who's given such a sign

d'amore, e de l'amor il dolce or gusta,
a cui gli affanni scorsi ed i perigli
fanno soave e dolce condimento;
ma restate con Dio, ch'io vo' seguire
il mio viaggio, e ritrovar Montano.

CORO

Non so se il molto amaro
che provato ha costui servendo, amando,
piangendo e disperando,
raddolcito puot'essere pienamente
d'alcun dolce presente;
ma, se più caro viene
e più si gusta dopo 'l male il bene,
io non ti cheggio, Amore,
questa beatitudine maggiore;
bea pur gli altri in tal guisa:
me la mia ninfa accoglia
dopo brevi preghiere e servir breve:
e siano i condimenti
de le nostre dolcezze
non sì gravi tormenti,
ma soavi disdegni
e soavi ripulse,
risse e guerre a cui segua,
reintegrando i cori, o pace o tregua.

IL FINE

of love, and of love tastes the sweet reward,
to whom the recent grief and dangers seem
a spice for love, filled with delight and sweet!
But may you go with God, for I must go
and find Montano. I bid you farewell.

CHORUS

I know not if the great
affliction he has suffered, serving long,
with tears, enduring wrong,
despairing, loving, could be quite put right
by some sweet present sight.
But if the good's more dear
and after suffering, more filled with cheer,
still I'd not be imbued
with such beatitude.
Let others be so blessed.
I'd rather win my nymph
with brief entreaties and with service brief.
And may the condiment
of our contentment be
not serious torment,
but games of gentle scorn
and sweet refusals, and
affrays and quarrels, which cease
and yield to hearts rejoined in truce and peace.

THE END

NOTES

1. That is, where the "icy grip" of l. 64 is "softest." Where that point might be is left to the reader's imagination.

2. The device of classical rhetoric used in ll. 43–46 is called *adunaton*. It reinforces an impossibility by comparing it to impossible events in nature.

3. Cynthia is the poetic name for Diana, goddess of the hunt and chastity. As goddess of the hunt, she carries a hunting horn and bow and arrows.

4. Marco Ariani assumes that the river is the Po, and that the action takes place nearby.

5. Pan was the god dear to the Arcadian shepherds.

6. Most of the characters have been identified with historical figures at the court of Alfonso II d'Este in Ferrara. Elpino was probably Giovan Battista Pigna, secretary to Alfonso; Licori was Lucrezia Bendidio, lady-in-waiting to Eleonora d'Este; Batto (l. 189) was Battista Guarini, author of the pastoral drama *Il Pastor Fido*; Tirsi was Tasso himself.

7. In mythology, Aurora was goddess of the dawn. Many critics have felt that the "grotto of Aurora" was a still-extant room in the d'Este palace in Ferrara, which was adorned with frescoes by Dosso Dossi depicting Aurora.

8. In this syntactically difficult passage (ll. 181–93), Elpino (Pigna) tells Licori (Lucrezia Bendidio) what he had heard Tirsi (Tasso) and Batto (Guarini) talking about, which was a story that Tirsi says he heard "from that great man who sang of arms and loves" (l. 192), that is from Ludovico Ariosto, whose epic poem *Orlando furioso* opens with a very similar line. Ariosto (1474–1533) left his "shepherd's pipes" (l. 193) or poetic ability to Tirsi (Tasso). Tasso's own great epic poem *Jerusalem Delivered* was modeled on Ariosto's work. All of this, of course, is being recounted to Silvia by Dafne.

9. The story comes from *Orlando furioso*, canto 34, l. 6ff.

10. The image of the mad lover carving poetry (or his beloved's name) on trees is endemic to both satiric and serious strains of the love tradition in Western literature, and a particularly famous and recent example would have been the action of the mad Orlando (caused by the disdain and loss of the beautiful Angelica) in *Orlando furioso*. The lines in italics

are very similar to the last tercet of Tasso's sonnet which begins "M'apre talor Madonna."

11. A forest of holm oaks.

12. Ircania is a part of Asia where the fiercest tigers were supposedly found.

13. Their "Muse" is their pursuit of poetry.

14. Certainly a curious comparison of Silvia to the poisonous snake that Cleopatra used to commit suicide. Some commentators explain that the ancients believed that magic could kill asps.

15. Several wise critics have identified several possible historical personages hiding under this name. Evidently it was someone Tasso did not like, possibly Sperone Speroni, who tried to dissuade Tasso from serving the d'Estes.

16. Literally, the "magazino de le ciance." *Ciance* (pl. *ciancia*) means gossip or nonsense; as the lines that follow show, this is a shop where nothing is what it seems to be. Yet *ciancia* is close to *cianca* (*leg* or *shank*), and even to *ciana* (*slut*), and there is probably a sexual undertone here, considering the scarcely disguised sexuality of the entire dialogue. According to the historically based allegory, Mopso (Sperone?) is warning Tirsi (Tasso) away from the d'Este court.

17. Mopso's warning begins in l. 235 and ends in l. 270; Tirsi's commentary on the warning begins in l.271 and ends with l.315. The city referred to is Ferrara; the "shop of nothing-is" (245) is the d'Este court. The "sirens, swans, and nymphs" (276) may be singers, poets, and court ladies. The "man, magnanimous and strong" (282) is Alfonso II. The "divinities; graceful, pretty nymphs"" (289) might be the princess sisters of Alfonso who lived at court: one was Eleonora, the beloved of Tasso. The "new Orfeos and Linuses" (290) are the court poets like Guarini and Pigna. Orpheus, the famous mythological musician whose music could move inanimate nature and even Hades itself, went to Hades to reclaim his dead wife Eurydice. Linus is a mythic poet and musician, son of Apollo. The references in ll.291–96 to Aurora, Phoebus (Apollo, god of poetry and music), and the Muses (the nine goddess–patrons of the arts) probably refer to the Dossi fresco. Elpino (Pigna) is seated among the Muses. Lines 301–6 probably indicate that Tasso was asked to turn to pastoral poetry ("to these retreats"), but he now has "more sonorous and proud a voice" and "trumpet tones," perhaps a reference to his martial epic, *Jerusalem Delivered.*

Notes

18. An old folk belief held that if someone was seen by a wolf before he saw the animal, it would make him mute. Perhaps so — it might eat him!

19. Literally *amoretti,* the "minor brothers" Cupid refers to in l.21 of the Prologue. They are "bowless, torchless" because no spur to love was needed in the Golden Age.

20. Honor, in other words, taught people to behave (speak, act) "properly," and not simply or naturally.

21. Silvia's name is "fitting" because it is related to *selva* (*woods, forest*), and thus refers to one who is wild or cruel. Another related word, *selvaggio,* can mean just that.

22. Ariani feels that this means that anyone who observes her when she is laughing and/or weeping would be so taken with her that he would die because he is unable to have her.

23. Tasso was in fact 29 in 1573 when *Aminta* was written.

24. The "one who here is thought a god" (l. 176) is Alfonso II, who is also referred to in l. 190. Lines 176–80 refer to his dukedom, which stretched from Comacchio on the Adriatic coast to Carrara on the Tyrrhenian Sea through alliance with the lords of Massa and Carrara. The Apennine range is between the two seas.

25. In other words, the Tigris River of Asia Minor would run through France, and the French Soane would run through Persia.

26. Not Athena, goddess of wisdom, nor her "School" — the famous School at Athens where Aristotle taught — nor Phoebus Apollo, god of poetry who sometimes made his home on Mount Helicon, home of the Muses, could teach of love as well as Cupid.

27. Bagpipes. Elpino (G. B. Pigna) composed eclogues, pastoral verse to be accompanied by bagpipes.

28. Diana.

29. The earliest editions of the play did not include this chorus, which was first published as a madrigal in 1587.

30. In Italian *pungere* (*to sting*) not only carries through the bee simile, but also has the sense of *to prick* and *to excite* or *stimulate.*

31. In some editions this character is identified simply as *Messenger.*

32. The four "P" gods are all associated with fecundity and pastoral sexuality. Pan and Pallas were minor gods associated with shepherds and their herds. Priapus, frequently a comic figure, was god of gardens and erections. Pomona was protectress of fruits and gardens. Hecate was Diana in her nighttime role as a hellish deity.

33. Silvia, that is.

34. Like the chorus that ends Act 3, this was perhaps written first for another purpose. It is the first stanza of a poem written for the marriage of Cesare d'Este and Virginia de' Medici. It also appears alone in a manuscript signed by the poet.

35. The one referred to is Licori (cf. 1.1.183ff.). In the allegory she is Pigna's lady, Lucrezia Bendidio.

36. Gentleness could suggest noble birth, as Ariani suggests, but only on the allegorical level, since literally they are shepherd and nymph. As defined by the *dolce stil nuovo* poets, however, gentleness was caused by love and had nothing to do with birth.

37. The "her" is Licori (Lucrezia), who had first entranced Tirsi (Tasso), and later Elpino (Pigna), who was free to love her when Tirsi left her.

38. Alphesibius is evidently a mythical healer, given the healing arts by Phoebus Apollo, who had also given Elpino the art of song. He might allude to Girolamo Brassauolo, a famous doctor at the court of Ferrara.

This Book Was Completed on June 25, 2000 at
Italica Press, New York, New York. It
Was Set in Garamond and Printed
on 60 lb Natural Paper
by BookSurge,
U. S. A./
E. U.